Martin Johnson Heade

MUSEUM OF FINE ARTS, BOSTON

in association with

YALE UNIVERSITY PRESS

New Haven and London

Martin Johnson Heade

THEODORE E. STEBBINS, JR.

with contributions by

JANET L. COMEY   KAREN E. QUINN   JIM WRIGHT

This exhibition was organized by the
Museum of Fine Arts, Boston.

Support for the exhibition and the accompanying
catalogue has been provided by the Henry Luce
Foundation, the United Company, and
the Vira I. Heinz Endowment.

Copyright ©1999
by Museum of Fine Arts, Boston
Library of Congress Catalog Card Number:
99-60202
ISBN 0-87846-466-2 paper
ISBN 0-300-081-693 cloth

FIRST EDITION

EXHIBITION DATES

Museum of Fine Arts, Boston
September 29, 1999–January 16, 2000

National Gallery of Art
February 13–May 7, 2000

Los Angeles County Museum of Art
May 28–August 17, 2000

FRONT COVER:
Giant Magnolias on a Blue Velvet Cloth
(cat. 71, detail)
National Gallery of Art, Washington, D.C.

FRONTISPIECE:
Seascape: Sunrise (cat. 2, detail)
Private Collection

BACK COVER:
The Stranded Boat (cat. 7, detail)
Museum of Fine Arts, Boston

Published in association with
Yale University Press, New Haven and London

PHOTOGRAPH CREDITS

*Most photographs were provided by the owners of
the works and are published by their permission.
Specific acknowledgments are as follows:*

© Addison Gallery of American Art, Phillips
    Academy, Andover, Massachusetts. All
    Rights Reserved: cat. 33.
Dirk Bakker: cats. 24, 35, 36, 37, 38, 39, 40, 41, 42,
    43, 44, 45, 46, 47, 48, 49, 50.
Brooklyn Museum of Art: cat. 10.
The Butler Institute of American Art: cat. 14.
The Currier Gallery of Art: cat. 18.
© 1995 The Detroit Institute of Arts: cat. 3,
    fig. 20.
William A. Farnsworth Library and Art Museum
    (William W. Cross, Warren, Maine): fig. 4.
M. Lee Fatheree: cat. 60.
Fine Arts Museums of San Francisco: cats. 6, 15.

The Flint Institute of Arts: cat. 12.
The Governor's Mansion, Austin, Texas: fig. 2.
Greg Heins: cat. 26.
Helga Photo Studio, Upper Montclair,
    N. J.: cat. 25, fig. 6.
© 1997 Los Angeles County Museum of Art: fig. 3.
© 1992 The Metropolitan Museum of Art: cat. 1.
© 1996 The Metropolitan Museum of Art: cat. 11.
Munson-Williams-Proctor Institute Museum of
    Art: fig. 22.
The Museum of American Art of the Pennsylvania
    Academy of the Fine Arts: cat. 23.
Museum of Art, Rhode Island School of Design
    (Cathy Carver): cat. 22.
Museum of Fine Arts, Boston: cats. 4, 5, 7, 16, 20,
    21, 29, 31, 56, 59, 61, 62, 64, 65, 66, 67, 68, 69,
    figs. 9, 10, 11, 12, 13, 15, 16, 17, 24, 25, 26, 27,
    28, 29, 30, 31, 32, 33, 34.
© 1998 Board of Trustees, National Gallery of
    Art, Washington: cats. 57, 71, fig. 21.
The Newark Museum: fig. 1.
R. W. Norton Art Gallery: cat. 70.
Philadelphia Museum of Art: cat. 28.
Reynolda House, Museum of American Art
    (Jackson Smith): cat. 58, fig. 23.
The Saint Louis Art Museum: cat. 27.
Shelburne Museum (Einars J. Mengis, staff
    photographer): figs. 8, 18.
The Toledo Museum of Art: fig. 37.
Paul Waldman: cat. 51.
Yale University Art Gallery: cat. 13.

PRINTED IN SINGAPORE

CONTENTS

LENDERS TO THE EXHIBITION

Addison Gallery of American Art, Phillips Academy,

    Andover, Massachusetts

Brooklyn Museum of Art

The Butler Institute of American Art, Youngstown, Ohio

Amon Carter Museum, Fort Worth, Texas

Theodore G. and Eleanor S. Congdon

The Currier Gallery of Art, Manchester, New Hampshire

The Detroit Institute of Arts

Mr. and Mrs. Stuart P. Feld

Jerald Dillon Fessenden

Fine Arts Museums of San Francisco

The Flint Institute of Arts, Flint, Michigan

Jo Ann and Julian Ganz, Jr.

Teresa Heinz and the Late Senator John Heinz

David L. Long and Elizabeth Valk Long

Mr. and Mrs. Henry Luce III

James W. and Frances G. McGlothlin

Manoogian Collection

The Metropolitan Museum of Art

The Museum of American Art of the Pennsylvania Academy

    of the Fine Arts, Philadelphia

Museum of Art, Rhode Island School of Design, Providence

Museum of Fine Arts, Boston

National Gallery of Art, Washington

The R. W. Norton Art Gallery, Shreveport, Louisiana

Roy Nutt Family Trust

James and Barbara Palmer

Philadelphia Museum of Art

Reynolda House, Museum of American Art, Winston-Salem,

    North Carolina

St. Augustine Historical Society

The Saint Louis Art Museum

Yale University Art Gallery

Anonymous private collections

DIRECTOR'S PREFACE

THE MUSEUM OF FINE ARTS has been dedicated to the study and exhibition of the work of Martin Johnson Heade since 1945, when the farsighted collector Maxim Karolik presented this institution with *Approaching Storm: Beach near Newport,* the first of many works by the painter to enter our collection. Now, 180 years after Heade's birth, we take pride in presenting what will surely be the most beautiful and most instructive exhibition of our time devoted to this master's work.

We are grateful for the excellent cooperation of the owners of Heade's paintings. Both private collectors and our museum colleagues have graciously shared with us the rarest and most beautiful of Heade's works. Special thanks are due to Richard Manoogian and to Jo Ann and Julian Ganz, Jr., for lending so extensively from their splendid collections. We are profoundly indebted to Mr. and Mrs. Richard Nash for their recent gift of two important Heade sketchbooks to our collection.

The whole project has been made possible by the superb generosity of the United Company, for which we offer profound thanks to Mr. and Mrs. James W. McGlothlin, and of the Vira I. Heinz Endowment, whose support was made possible through the kindness of James M. Walton, Chairman, and of Teresa Heinz. The catalogue has been underwritten by an important grant received from the Henry Luce Foundation, whom we thank most sincerely. The Luce Foundation has an outstanding record of support for important exhibitions in the American field, and we are proud to have earned its assistance once again. We are especially grateful to Time, Inc., particularly to Elizabeth Valk Long and David L. Long, for the generous and highly effective media sponsorship of this exhibition.

The exhibition has been curated by Theodore E. Stebbins, Jr., Acting Chair, Art of the Americas, who here makes another significant contribution to Heade scholarship. He has worked in close collaboration with Karen Quinn and Janet Comey in American Paintings, and with Jim Wright, Eyk and Rose-Marie van Otterloo Conservator of Paintings at the Museum of Fine Arts. The production of the catalogue was expertly overseen by Cynthia Purvis in the Office of Scholarly Publications. Patricia Loiko, Registrar, and Katherine Getchell, Deputy Director for Curatorial Affairs, managed all aspects of the exhibition. We are also grateful to Gilian Shallcross Wohlauer in the Department of Education and Public Programs and Susan Wong in Design.

Finally, I extend very special thanks to Earl A. Powell III, Director of the National Gallery of Art, and Graham W. J. Beal, Director of the Los Angeles County Museum of Art, for sharing this exhibition and enabling a nationwide audience to enjoy the paintings of Martin Johnson Heade.

MALCOLM ROGERS
Ann and Graham Gund Director

ACKNOWLEDGMENTS

THE LAST RETROSPECTIVE EXHIBITION of the work of Martin Johnson Heade took place thirty years ago, and in the intervening years countless people have assisted our work on this painter with great kindness. I am profoundly grateful to all those who helped in ways both large and small. This project has particularly benefited from the generous assistance of the owners of Heade's work, private and public, of the dealers who have handled it, and of numerous scholars in the field. Museum curators, registrars, photographic departments, and others have responded promptly and graciously to our numerous requests. Librarians and their staffs have been unfailingly forthcoming. Most important for this exhibition, private collectors and museums have been extremely generous in granting us the loans of many of Heade's greatest paintings. To all we extend our sincerest thanks.

The Heade exhibition of 1969 owed a great deal to William H. Gerdts, and it is gratifying to say that on this occasion, I am once again deeply grateful for his help. Professor Gerdts has shared his superb library, very kindly read an early draft of my essay, and has been helpful in many ways. Franklin Kelly, Curator of American and British Paintings at the National Gallery of Art, has also been a perfect colleague, aiding in the selection of the exhibition and reading an early draft of the catalogue.

Jo Ann and Julian Ganz, Jr., friends of many years, have been highly supportive of this project. Richard Manoogian, the preeminent Heade collector of our time, has played a crucial role in the formation of this exhibition. My late friend Robert C. Vose, Jr., acted with typical magnanimity in allowing me to pore over the Vose Gallery records at great length, and in sharing much other information. The generous gift from Mr. and Mrs. Richard Nash of Heade's Brazil/London journal to the Museum of Fine Arts has been of crucial importance to our work. Finally, I am deeply appreciative of the friendship and support of Mr. and Mrs. James W. McGlothlin and of Teresa Heinz.

With regard to our research, we offer special thanks to Gustavo Romero, Keeper of Orchids, Museum of Comparative Zoology, Harvard University; Judith A. Warnement, Librarian, Botany Libraries, Harvard University; Stephen Scanniello, Rosarian; Philip Pryde; Alfred C. Harrison, The North Point Gallery, San Francisco; Col. Merl M. Moore, Jr.; Dorothy-Lee Jones, Jones Museum of Glass and Ceramics, Sebago, Maine; and the staffs at the Archives of American Art, John Carter Brown Library, Brown University, Beinecke Library, Yale University, and Houghton Library, Harvard University. We are also grateful to Kevin Avery, Joan Barnes, Jerry Bloomer, Jonathan Boos, Holly Capozzi, Helen Cooper, Page Edwards, Ilene Fort, Jane Gallup, Whitney Ganz, Mike Hammer, Samantha Kimpel, Susan Nalezyty, Susan Roberts-Manganelli, Maureen O'Brien, Dana Pilson, Darrel Sewell, P. Andrew Spahr, Charles Sterling,

Kurt Sundstrom, Michael Altman, Timothy A. Eaton, Sue and Stuart Feld, Martha Fleishman, James and Frederick Hill, Ira Spanierman, Bruce Weber, and Island Weiss.

From the beginning, this project has been a joint venture with the department of Paintings Conservation at the Museum of Fine Arts, and we deeply appreciate the contributions of our colleagues Jean Woodward and Elizabeth Leto Fulton. For indispensable research assistance we are grateful to Leslie Furth and Ellen Roberts, both Muriel G. S. Lewis Fellows, to Giuseppina (Pepi) Marchetti Franchi and Karen Pfefferle, both Barbara Fish Lee Fellows, in Art of the Americas, and to Susan C. Ricci. We owe profound thanks as well to Cynthia Purvis for overseeing production of this book, to Susan Marsh for her sympathetic design, to Fronia W. Simpson for her fine editing, and to Katherine Getchell and Patricia Loiko for managing all aspects of the exhibition.

At the Museum of Fine Arts we also thank especially Malcolm Rogers, Ann and Graham Gund Director, and Katherine Getchell, Deputy Director for Curatorial Affairs, for their support of this project; Joanne Donovan and Maureen Melton, William Morris Hunt Library; Nicole Luongo, Karen Otis, Mary Sluskonis, Jennifer Reilly, Tom Lang, Gary Ruuska, Greg Heins, and John Woolf, Photographic Services; Dacey Sartor, Scholarly Publications; Paul Bessire and Jennifer Cooper, Development; Roy Perkinson, Gail English, Sue Reed, and Shelley Langdale, Department of Prints, Drawings and Photographs; Diane Dalton and Jackie Lane, Ladies Committee; David Sturtevant, Rights and Reproductions; Elizabeth Ann Coleman and Lauren Whitley, Textiles; Gerald Ward, Andy Haines and Julia McCarthy, Art of the Americas; Leane Coppola and Rhona Macbeth, Paintings Conservation; Gilian Shallcross Wohlauer, Education; Dawn Griffin, Public Relations and Marketing and Susan Wong, Design.

Finally, it is hard to find words to thank my three collaborators on this exhibition. Karen Quinn has been working with me on Martin Johnson Heade for twelve years; through her hard work and high standards she has made many crucial contributions to this project. Janet Comey has played numerous key roles, as researcher, writer, indexer, and organizer, and she has my profound thanks. Finally, Jim Wright, one of the nation's leading conservators of paintings, has been an indispensable partner, and I am grateful to him for devoting so much time and attention to this fascinating American painter.

THEODORE E. STEBBINS, JR.

INTRODUCTION

MARTIN JOHNSON HEADE had the longest career and produced perhaps the most varied body of work of any American painter of the nineteenth century. Born in 1819 in rural Pennsylvania, he had begun to paint by about 1837, when he was eighteen, and he was still working at his easel a few weeks before his death in Florida in September 1904, some sixty-seven years later. Though he won only a minor reputation in his own day and after his death was completely forgotten for many decades, he is now rightly regarded as an artist of great significance and originality, and as the only American whose landscapes and still lifes are equally powerful.

Heade was a quintessential doubter in every aspect of his life, whether in politics or art, signing many articles for *Forest and Stream* and other publications "Didymus," after the apostle Thomas. He traveled on his own over the world, a completely self-reliant American. The son of a farmer, he became a hunter and fisherman who deeply loved nature and the countryside while learning the ways of the city well enough to survive as a painter for more than six decades. He was a land speculator but one who frequently disparaged the rich. Heade was a nonjoiner in an age of artists' clubs and associations, yet he could count among his friends and patrons not only Frederic E. Church and Mark Twain but also such notable clergy as Henry Ward Beecher, Noah Schenck, and Thomas March Clark; leading scientists including Louis Agassiz and Eben J. Loomis; tycoons such as Cyrus Field and Henry Morrison Flagler; and important civic leaders such as Fairman Rogers and John Russell Bartlett. Heade was always an unconventional figure, in the ways he thought, in the manner in which he functioned in the world and lived his life — especially in his highly original approach to painting — and he was always fiercely proud of his independence.

Heade apparently learned the rudiments of his craft from his neighbor in Bucks County, the folk artist Edward Hicks, who is well remembered today as the painter of many versions of *The Peaceable Kingdom*. By 1839 Heade was capable enough to paint *Portrait of a Young Lady* (fig. 1) in the flat, conceptual manner of the nonacademic painter, and in 1841 he began his professional career when *Portrait of a Little Girl* (unlocated) was shown in the annual exhibition at the Pennsylvania Academy of the Fine Arts in Philadelphia. He moved away from his father's home and set off on his own about 1843, when he moved to New York for the first time.

For the next fifteen years, Heade traveled the length and breadth of America and journeyed to Europe as well, learning his trade while painting portraits, genre scenes, and copies of famous American and European portraits. An itinerant, Heade worked in Brooklyn for a time, then — in a high point of his early career — went to Washington, D.C., in 1846 to paint the

Fig. 1. *Portrait of a Young Lady*, 1839, oil on canvas. Collection of The Newark Museum, Newark, New Jersey, Gift of Mr. and Mrs. Stephen Sloan, 1986 (86.268).

Fig. 2. *General Samuel Houston*, 1846, oil on canvas. The Governor's Mansion, Austin, Texas.

hero of the Battle of San Jacinto, General Samuel Houston, from life (fig. 2). In this competent, well-modeled work, Heade demonstrates a new mastery. In 1848–49, thanks to the generosity of his father, he spent two years abroad, largely in Rome; on his return he painted in St. Louis, Chicago, Trenton, Providence, Mobile, and New Orleans, among other places. Yet a decade after painting Houston, Heade was still a journeyman painter at best; in neither his portraits, genre scenes, nor

copies had he acquired anything more than a modest competence. Regarding his early work, it should also be noted that only about forty of the figurative pictures are known today. Judging from his prolificacy later on, one might guess that Heade painted two to four hundred works between 1839 and 1858; thus the vast majority of the early oeuvre remains to be identified, or has been lost forever.

Heade became interested in landscape during the mid-

Fig. 3. *Rhode Island Shore*, 1858, oil on canvas. Los Angeles County Museum of Art, Gift of Charles C. and Elma Ralphs Shoemaker, AC1994.152.6.

1850s, and in the summer of 1857 he went to sketch in the White Mountains of New Hampshire, where he met the well-established landscapists John F. Kensett and Benjamin Champney. However, his progress was slow. He wrote to his friend John Russell Bartlett, "I find landscape painting not quite so easy as I supposed."[1] A year later he did the wisest thing an aspiring landscape artist could have done: he moved back to New York and in November 1858 secured the last available stu-dio in the new Tenth Street Studio Building. Here he found himself working alongside the leading painters of the Hudson River School; Church and Sanford Gifford were at work in the same building, while Kensett and Asher B. Durand had studios nearby. Heade particularly admired Church's work, and the two became lifelong friends and correspondents. Heade's art changed dramatically at this time: he gave up figurative work and began to specialize in landscape and still life. In addition, his work quickly became known in New York and in the many cities around the country where he exhibited regularly.

Heade's first few landscapes, of late 1858 and early 1859,

make use of traditional Hudson River School formats, in which tall trees frame one side of the composition in the "Claudian" manner, and the eye is led toward distant hills and water. Heade's *Rhode Island Shore*, 1858 (fig. 3), uses these conventional devices, while also presaging almost all of his subsequent concerns as a landscapist: long shadows suggest his devotion to the depiction of light and time of day; a single haystack on the left is a harbinger of many future paintings; and sailboats on the expansive bay demonstrate his nascent interest in marine painting.

By late 1859, however, Heade had discarded convention as he developed his own approach to landscape painting, taking elements of the style and practice of the Hudson River School and adapting them to his own vision. In this year he produced his first marine paintings (including *Approaching Thunder Storm*, cat. 1) and his earliest marsh scenes, while he continued to paint some traditional landscapes as well. This established the pattern for the rest of his working life: of the landscapes he produced during his mature career, from 1859 to 1904, about half are marsh or swamp scenes, one quarter are seashore views, and the remaining quarter represent typical Hudson River School compositions depicting mountain valleys, wooded pastures, and the like. In each of these formats, and in still life as well, Heade made paintings of astonishing originality.

He first mastered the shore scene, making geometrically simple works in which great waves break on sandy shores or thunderstorms loom offshore over ink black water. These works, which took up much of his time between 1859 and 1863, owe something to Church and perhaps to Kensett as well, but they are easily distinguishable in their plainness — the waves especially demonstrating Heade's roots in folk art — and their bleakness. There are certain parallels between Heade's work and Fitz Hugh Lane's, especially in 1863, but Lane was a member of an earlier generation, an optimistic painter of the age of sail, and the two painters' works express very different visions. Heade's marines (especially the thunderstorms) have also been thought to express his own feelings, and perhaps also reflect the national anguish, about the Civil War. Heade was very much a Northern partisan; even on his long trip abroad of 1863–65, he expressed his deep concern for what he called "our unfortunate country," and he talked about the war with Charles Francis Adams, the American minister in London. His fears for the Union long went unassuaged, and in July 1864 he wrote, "Affairs begin to assume a dark aspect, and almost for the first time I'm giving way to despair."[2]

Heade painted numerous series of works. Some of the series were short-lived and consist of fewer than half a dozen explorations of a given theme, while others — such as the large-scale marine pictures discussed above — were made over a decade or more. Of all his series, however, the longest lasting was the one devoted to the northeastern salt marsh; this is the subject of nearly 120 surviving paintings, and doubtless there were once many more. Heade painted the marsh in the way that Thoreau wrote of Walden Pond, describing every detail and every nuance of an area that to most seemed mundane and forgettable. The marsh was a natural region, yet it was man-made as well, for the numerous large haystacks there speak to the skill and hard labor of the farmer. The marsh seems also to have been an important site in Heade's mind; in it he could be alone — observing, sketching, painting — and in his paintings of it he could celebrate his love of the country and a yearning for his own youth. Frequently in the marsh scenes he includes a man and a boy — perhaps standing for his father and himself — who fish, tend cattle, or rake or stack hay. He painted the

marsh at dawn and at sunset, and under every kind of atmospheric condition; gray skies and rain clouds threaten, spots of sunlight move across the level grasses, a small boat drifts silently upriver. Eastern salt marshes have a sameness of appearance, whether at Newbury, Marshfield, Ipswich, or Lynn, all in Massachusetts, or in Connecticut, but every painting of the marsh was a pictorial experiment. Each one is full of changes and pentimenti, as Jim Wright describes in his essay below. The measuring of space and the rhythm of haystacks and winding rivers receding toward a distant horizon never ceased to fascinate Heade. There are failures in the series, pictures where he could not work out certain problems, but there are never duplicates.

If the paintings of the shore as well as the more conventional compositions that he continued to make, such as *Lake George* (cat. 20), might lead one to think of Heade as a Hudson River School painter, the marshes make it clear that he was not. Church, Kensett, Durand, and the others frequently worked outdoors on their summer trips making pencil and oil sketches to help them later paint specific topography and close-up details accurately, and they painted the hallowed sites such as Niagara Falls and the White Mountains. Heade responded to nature differently. Much as he tried, he could not accept the well-established iconography of picturesque America or of the tropics. He sketched outdoors, but once he had a satisfactory rendering of a haystack or an orchid, he would use it again and again, the way a folk painter would use a stencil. When he traveled in 1860 to Vermont, where Church had found so many subjects for paintings, Heade came across none. As he wrote his friend Bartlett from Rutland, "It's a little singular that I've seen nothing yet that I cared to sketch!"[3] Heade's marshes were as pioneering as his orchids, for both show him rejecting,

as David Miller has put it, the "high Romantic iconography, associated, for example, with the Hudson River school and . . . the moral allegory and aesthetic criteria that underlay it."[4] As American perceptions of nature changed from the Emersonian to the Darwinian, new kinds of paintings were needed, and Heade was among the first to provide them. Mark Twain was a spokesman for the new, urbanized nation in the post–Civil War "Gilded Age," and he — not coincidentally — was an admirer of Heade's work and the owner of one of the marsh scenes. Both Heade and Twain were caustic critics of materialism who nonetheless found ways to make the system work for them. Both were skeptics and wits who felt equal to anyone; both carried with them memories of having grown up in rural surroundings beside a great river. And both were travelers who in times of doubt would "light out for the territory," as Huck Finn did.[5]

The way Heade made his living suggests his acumen in dealing with the urban world. Every year from 1859 until the late 1880s he would arrange to have his work exhibited and offered for sale in multiple cities throughout the nation. Moving as often as he did enabled him to form relationships with dealers, exhibition officials, and perhaps with collectors and press as well, in numerous places. This is not to suggest that his moves were part of a plan, but simply that he made his restlessness work for him. His prices never reached the levels that Bierstadt's or Church's attained; rather, they seem instead to have remained about the same throughout his career. On the average he realized between $100 and $200 per painting ($2,000–4,000 in today's money), which meant that he needed to sell ten to fifteen pictures a year to meet his expenses. In one typical year, 1868, for example, he sent *Thunder Storm on Narragansett Bay* (cat. 8) to exhibitions at the

Brooklyn Art Association and then at the National Academy of Design, while other pictures were shown at the Pennsylvania Academy, the Utica Art Association, the Chicago Academy of Design, the Fine Arts Academy in Buffalo, the Derby Gallery in New York, and the Cincinnati Academy. A decade later, in 1878, the venues had changed but the level of activity remained the same; that year he exhibited individual works at the National Academy of Design, the Massachusetts Charitable Mechanic Association in Boston, Gill's Gallery in Springfield, Massachusetts, and in addition sold ten paintings, including landscapes, marines, and still lifes, at O'Brien's Art Gallery in Chicago.

Heade must have had extraordinary energy. He painted between fifteen and twenty-five works annually, sometimes undoubtedly more; he arranged for the shipping, framing, and exhibition of his works; he corresponded regularly with friends and business colleagues; he published poetry during the 1840s, articles in the *Providence Journal* in the 1850s, many pieces on hunting, fishing, and nature in his last quarter century in *Forest and Stream*, and doubtless a good deal else still unknown to us. Heade moved around constantly on long trips and shorter ones; and he found time wherever he went to go hunting and fishing, two activities he was passionate about. He must have been a very active, highly competent, clear-minded individual, and he was confident of his ability to function well both in the outdoors he had revered since youth (proudly acknowledging his "reputation for skill in shooting," for example) and in the complex urban world on which he depended for his livelihood. Once when Church forgot to tell him something important, he wrote another friend saying, "Strange that artists are all so forgetful, except myself."[6]

As inventive as Heade's landscapes are, it could be argued that his still lifes are even more so. He began painting them in New York in 1859, just as with the seascapes and marsh scenes, and quickly gained mastery of the new genre. In November 1859 a Boston critic commented that several of Heade's floral compositions "betray a most careful and earnest study of nature" and then concluded: "they are the best specimens of flower painting we have ever seen."[7] His earliest series of still lifes was devoted to compositions depicting roses, lilies, heliotrope, and other species standing in a variety of plain and decorated vases. Even though these pictures have a traditional look and relate to work being done by his contemporaries in America, including George C. Lambdin and George H. Hall, they are nonetheless unmistakably Heades. Both the flowers and the vases are more sensuous than in the work of others; as with the landscapes, the still lifes seem redolent with memory and meaning.

Doubtless inspired by Church's example, Heade traveled to South and Central America three times, going to Brazil to paint the hummingbirds in 1863–64, taking a brief trip to Nicaragua in 1866, then making a longer journey to Colombia, Panama, and Jamaica in 1870. In Rio de Janeiro in 1864 he exhibited twelve of his small hummingbird paintings (*The Gems of Brazil*) along with a view of Rio and was honored by the forward-looking emperor, Dom Pedro II. In his journal Heade matter-of-factly recorded several discussions with the emperor about his hummingbirds, expressing no surprise that a monarch would take an interest in his work. Later in the year he traveled to London to have his paintings chromolithographed for his proposed book on the hummingbirds of Brazil. The project was never completed, whether due to a lack of subscribers, the inadequacy of the prints, or some combination of the two, but Heade in London in 1864–65 nonetheless enjoyed the most enthusiastic patronage of his career, leasing "one of the finest studios in London," exhibiting what he considered "a smashing landscape" at the Royal Academy, and selling numerous works including a Brazilian scene for $900 and a pair of hummingbird pictures for $375. He wrote Bartlett, "My success . . . has almost bewildered me, & I can only account for it by my being in an entirely new line."[8]

Even more of a "new line" was the long series of paintings depicting the hummingbirds with passion flowers or orchids, which he began in 1870. These works combine traditional features of both landscape and still life along with elements of ornithological and botanical illustration. One seeks in vain for direct precedents for these astonishing works within either American or European art. Where Church described the grandeur of South America for the pre–Civil War audience in huge paintings filled with Ruskinian detail, Heade summarizes the tropical experience — the heat, the alluring sensuality, the mesmerizing beauty — in compositions of modest size. As Katherine E. Manthorne has written, in such works "microcosm becomes macrocosm."[9] These paintings, like those of the northern marshes, do not celebrate place, like Church's, but rather evoke the ineluctable but almost imperceptible movement of time in nature. If Cole and Church depicted nature as a constant and time as reflecting man's "voyage of life" on earth, for Heade and his artistic generation man is only a bystander, and nature — nature the actor — takes center stage. As Ella Foshay has suggested, these paintings more than any other in American art seem to reflect the acceptance of the new worldview represented by Darwinism.[10]

Heade reinvented himself again in 1883 when he moved to St. Augustine, Florida, and then married. There he found domestic tranquillity and permanence, and there his wander-

Cat. 69 (detail)

ings stopped. In Henry Morrison Flagler Heade found a generous and admiring patron; and he was honored in St. Augustine as the dean of the local artists. In his sixties and seventies he might have settled for repeating earlier compositions, but instead he responded to the Florida landscape and to the state's flowers and fruit with several new series of works. In painting the St. Johns River and the southern swamps, Heade reverted to canvases of larger size and to compositions reminiscent of those of the Hudson River School. Foregrounds now depict calm, murky river waters, while palms and cypresses lead the eye toward distant horizons. The tension one feels in the early marines and the clarity evident in the northern marshes have been replaced by density and stasis; Heade's Florida landscapes are damp, turgid, unknowable, and unchanging.

An even greater change is seen in Heade's Florida still lifes. New subjects and his own new life together led him to reinvent his art once again. The late still lifes, especially the Cherokee roses and the magnolias, are the opposite of what one would expect of an aging artist in semiretirement. In his other late work, when he would paint an orchid or a Newbury marsh, Heade's brushwork was looser than before, his execution often sloppier. But during the very same years, when he depicted the flowers of Florida, his touch seems surer than ever before in his life. The famous reclining magnolias demonstrate another invention of Heade's: he had always painted flowers for their feminine qualities, but now the blossoms, reclining luxuriantly on red or blue velvet, take on the ivory skin color and assume the very poses of the alluring woman herself. Moving beyond the passionate sensuality of the orchids, the artist now came to paint a luxuriant sexuality.

In these final paintings, Heade was again out of step with the stylistic mainstream. He had begun by spending twenty years painting portraits and copies, while missing the heyday of the Hudson River School and the heroic genre paintings of George Caleb Bingham and William Sidney Mount. Then when he found his true calling, about 1860, his inventiveness in the marsh paintings and the orchid and passion flower series demonstrated his keen (though perhaps unconscious) awareness of the period's most important intellectual currents. Finally, at the end of his life, again paying little attention to the fashionable, and making not the slightest concession to the popular new styles coming to America from France and Germany, he employed a now out-of-date realist style to produce some of the most remarkable still lifes in our history.

In all the work of his artistic maturity, Heade was a romantic masquerading as a realist. He studied the hummingbirds, the orchids, and the passion flowers with the eye of a naturalist, just as he sketched the landscapes of the Northeast, Florida, and Brazil using the methods of the topographical painter. Yet in each genre, the paintings have more to do with memory than with fact; they speak less to keenness of observation than to the richness of the painter's imagination.

THEODORE E. STEBBINS, JR.

NOTES

1. Martin Johnson Heade to John Russell Bartlett, July 28, 1857, Bartlett Papers, John Carter Brown Library, Brown University, Providence, Rhode Island.
2. Heade to Bartlett, July 25, 1864.
3. Heade to Bartlett, July 23, 1860.
4. David C. Miller, *Dark Eden: The Swamp in Nineteenth-Century American Culture* (New York: Cambridge University Press, 1989), p. 1.
5. Mark Twain, *The Adventures of Huckleberry Finn* (1884; New York: Harper & Brothers, 1912), p. 405.
6. Martin Johnson Heade to John Russell Bartlett, September 30 [1867], John Russell Bartlett Papers, MSS 286, Rhode Island Historical Society.
7. "Art Items," *Boston Transcript*, November 1, 1859, p. 2.
8. Heade to Bartlett, September 2, 1864 (as in note 1).
9. Katherine Emma Manthorne, *Tropical Renaissance: North American Artists Exploring Latin America, 1839–1879* (Washington, D.C., and London: Smithsonian Institution Press, 1989), p. 129.
10. Ella Milbank Foshay, *Nineteenth-Century American Flower Painting and the Botanical Sciences*, Ph.D. diss., Columbia University, 1979 (Ann Arbor, Mich.: UMI Research Press, 1981).

SEASCAPES

AFTER SPENDING TWO DECADES as a figurative painter specializing in portraits and genre scenes, Heade, late in 1858, moved to New York, where he quickly became a painter of land- and seascapes. Between 1859 and 1868 he painted numerous marine pictures, often shore scenes with breaking waves, with many of them coming in the first four years of this period.

Heade's earliest seascapes date from 1859. *Storm Clouds on the Coast* (fig. 4) establishes his basic compositional scheme with its sharp horizon, its depiction of the sun breaking through the clouds of a receding storm, and its dark sea crashing on a rocky shore in the foreground. The scene includes tall framing trees at the left, a traditional compositional element of the Hudson River School and one Heade would soon reject. A second, presumably later, picture of the same year, *Approaching Thunder Storm* (cat. 1), is more developed. The calm water of the bay (representing part of Narragansett Bay near Bristol, Rhode Island) is almost black, and the pale green spits of land and the single white sail dramatically contrast with both the water and the ominous, dark storm clouds above. Though this work is transitional — the emphasis on foreground elements, including a sail drying on the rocks at left and the young man and his dog at right, would be greatly reduced in future compositions — it still represents an extraordinary breakthrough for an unknown painter who was new both to New York and to

Fig. 4. *Storm Clouds on the Coast*, 1859, oil on canvas. William A. Farnsworth Library and Art Museum, Rockland, Maine, Museum purchase, 1965.

such subjects. Contemporary critics recognized its quality, one writing that "the ominous hush . . . the pale foreground, the black water, the dread feeling in the coming storm, and the homely and careless fisherman . . . present an effect that is rare and true."[1]

Two paintings of 1860 fully established Heade's approach to marine painting. *Low Tide* (fig. 5) and *Seascape: Sunrise* (cat. 2) are both ambitious, large-scale works (each being about

Fig. 5. *Low Tide*, 1860, oil on canvas. Private Collection, Providence, R.I.

28 x 50 in.) representing the coast at Newport, Rhode Island; they are alike in their broad, flat horizons, which divide the composition nearly equally between sea and sky, in their simple foregrounds of rocks and seaweed, and in their lack of anecdote. *Low Tide* pictures a completely benign sea at midday, while *Seascape: Sunrise* represents the dark sea rolling in large crests onto a rocky shore at dawn.

Heade continued this series with the Detroit Institute's *Seascape: Sunset*, 1861 (cat. 3), and the Boston Museum's *Approaching Storm: Beach near Newport* (cat. 4), which on stylistic grounds seems datable to 1861–63. Both works rely on *Seascape: Sunrise* as an antecedent, with *Seascape: Sunset* employing the same devices of a dark green sea and a multihued sky marked by red clouds on the horizon, while *Approaching Storm* further develops the theme of powerful foaming waves rolling up on the shore. Barbara Novak has written of Heade's roots in folk painting and the continuing "primitivism" of some of his mature work.[2] In these shore scenes, the awkward but compelling waves are painted both literally — as if the white impasto could convince us of the reality of their foaming crests — and decoratively, for the sake of their sinuous curves, as one would expect of an artist with a background in the folk tradition. A contemporary critic noticed this quality when he wrote in 1860 of *Approaching Thunder Storm*: "At first glance the effect is crude, [but] a closer examination declares it one of the best paintings in the exhibition."[3]

One inevitably wonders how Heade came to paint such pictures, and where he learned this style. He began to depict the sea shortly after moving in November 1858 into the Tenth Street Studio Building in New York, where for the first time he

Fig. 6. Frederic E. Church
(1826–1900), *Beacon, off Mount
Desert Island*, 1851, oil on canvas.
Private Collection.

became intimately acquainted with the leading New York painters and their work. Heade was quickly impressed with the work of Frederic E. Church, particularly admiring his recently completed *Niagara*, 1857 (Corcoran Gallery of Art, Washington, D.C.).[4] Church's picture is notable for the simplicity of its extended horizontal composition and for the way it depicts sky and water divided by a long, flat horizon — all elements found in Heade's seascapes. Moreover, earlier marine paintings by Church provide a likely source for Heade's burgeoning interest in such subjects. Church's seascapes such as *The Wreck*, 1852 (The Parthenon, Nashville, Tenn.), or *Beacon, off Mount Desert Island*, 1851 (fig. 6), are dramatic twilight scenes with flat horizons extending across the composition, much as Heade's would do. Heade in this period emulated Church's palette and technique, as Jim Wright discusses in his essay in

this catalogue, and it is reasonable to think he might have been influenced by the younger man's compositions as well.

Heade's early marines present a harsher view of nature than do Church's, with compositions both more austere and more abstract. Church's pictures satisfied the common critical demand of the day for "truth to nature," while Heade's often did not. One critic admired the sky in *Seascape: Sunset* as "a picture by itself," but the work was ruined for him by the lack of any reflection of the twilit sky on the dark sea below, a lack he damned as "untrue."[5]

In 1862–63 Heade continued his series of shoreline views. First he would typically sketch the view in pencil, following Hudson River School practice, and then he might execute it in a small but finished picture of about 12 by 24 inches; if he liked it, or perhaps if he received an order, he would then make a large version suitable for exhibition. The small *Dawn*, 1862 (cat. 5), and the larger *Twilight, Singing Beach*, 1863 (cat. 6), two views of Boston's North Shore, show his response to the earlier criticism: both the former, with its atypical warm light, and the latter, with its cool gray sea tinged with reflections of the raspberry-colored horizon, demonstrate the painter's new abilities in uniting sky and water.[6]

In 1863 Heade experimented with a new vision of the sea. John Wilmerding has long postulated that at about this time Heade may have met Fitz Hugh Lane (1804-1865), the Gloucester marine painter, or at least had come to know Lane's work.[7] This seems possible, and may account for Heade's briefly taking up a more traditional approach to the subject. In any case, Heade for a few months became a painter of fog and haze on the water, subjects Lane had depicted frequently. Heade's *Hazy Sunrise at Sea*, 1863 (Shelburne Museum, Shelburne, Vt.), and *The Stranded Boat*, 1863 (cat. 7), portray ships emerging from a bank of fog. Both are moody and profound works, and both are pictorially convincing in their depiction of ships moving across calm seas in nearly impenetrable haze. No nineteenth-century exhibition records or criticism of these pictures has been found, but there is no reason to think that contemporary observers would have found them "untrue," which makes Heade's failure to produce any more work in this vein all the more puzzling.

Between September 1863 and late 1866, Heade was traveling extensively in the tropics, and his production of marine paintings diminished as other interests became dominant. However, in 1867 he executed a large view of Point Judith, now lost,[8] and in 1868 painted *Thunder Storm on Narragansett Bay* (cat. 8), the key picture in the rediscovery of Heade that occurred during the 1940s (see Stebbins's essay, "Picturing Heade," in this catalogue). This is now — with *Approaching Storm: Beach near Newport* — perhaps the best-known of all his works. The two paintings, which are often discussed together, have many obvious similarities, both portraying dark, dramatic storms over black water and both making telling use of white sails as compositional devices to mark a measured recession into the distance. At the same time, there are important distinctions between them. *Approaching Storm* is very much part of Heade's early series of somewhat primitive, abstracted, visionary views of the sea. The rocky shore to the left, lit by a pale green light, appears unpopulated and daunting, and the breaking waves look schematized and frozen; overall, the view seems compelling but inaccessible. *Thunder Storm on Narragansett Bay*, on the other hand, like its direct antecedent *Approaching Thunder Storm*, 1859, and like *The Stranded Boat*, 1863, is accessible; judging from the houses and towns on the distant shore, its locale is a real one, and one could easily walk down the shore to the sand spit, where several figures move slowly away from their boat. Though the storm is frightening, even cataclysmic, Heade suggests that the universe, even if fearsome, is essentially rational and knowable. The right-hand boat approaches land under power of both sail and oars; the one at far left is beginning to lower its sail, while the sloop at left center has been safely beached. One man finishes lowering the sail while other members of the crew, a man and boy, carry in the oars. As J. Gray Sweeney has written, *Thunder Storm on Narragansett Bay* suggests a secularized and modernized version of Thomas Cole's famous series, *The Voyage of Life*.[9]

Heade continued to paint the sea after 1868, but never again did he attempt such an unconventional picture as *Thunder Storm on Narragansett Bay*. Contemporary critics reacted

Fig. 7. *Thimble Islands near New Haven*, 1875, oil on canvas. Private Collection.

Fig. 8. *Thimble Island*, about 1875–76, oil on canvas. Shelburne Museum, Shelburne, Vermont, 27.1.2-66.

negatively to its mixing of dramatic rainstorm, heightened stillness, and vibrant contrasts of white sails against dark water and sky. Comments ranged from "hard and chilling," "very faulty," to simply "bad."[10] Perhaps discouraged, Heade painted no further thunderstorm-at-sea compositions, and his output of marine views in general dwindled over the next decade before halting altogether. During the 1870s he painted two more large pictures, *Coast of Newport*, 1874 (private collection), and *Off the Coast of California*, about 1875 (unlocated), which was exhibited at the Philadelphia Centennial Exposition of 1876.

Finally, during the 1870s Heade produced a small group of quiet marine views, which are almost devoid of anecdotal detail.[11] *Becalmed, Long Island Sound* (cat. 9) is one of three small canvases Heade executed after a trip to the Connecticut coast late in the summer of 1875. The other two, *Thimble Islands near New Haven*, 1875 (fig. 7), and *Thimble Island*, about 1875-76 (fig. 8), depict low tide; in these works Heade contrasted dark rocks in the foreground to the subtly lit sky, and boats dot the horizon. In *Becalmed*, however, the tide has moved in and covered the rocks, and only two sailboats, off-center, attempt to sail the still waters.[12] The luminous sky reflected in the undisturbed water creates one of Heade's most quiet, harmonious compositions.

KAREN E. QUINN

NOTES

1. "National Academy of Design: Fourth Gallery," *Home Journal* (New York), May 5, 1860, p. 2.

2. Barbara Novak, *American Painting of the Nineteenth Century* (New York: Praeger, 1969), pp. 127-128.

3. "National Academy of Design: Fourth Gallery."

4. "Church's picture of Niagara far exceeds my expectations; & I don't wonder that Ruskin, after looking at it half an hour could only utter 'marvelous!' " Martin Johnson Heade to John Russell Bartlett, November 4, 1858, Bartlett Papers, John Carter Brown Library, Brown University, Providence, Rhode Island.

5. *New-York Daily Tribune*, March 27, 1861, p. 8.

6. For a discussion of Heade's North Shore paintings, see Sarah Cash, "Singing Beach, Manchester: Four Newly Identified Paintings of the North Shore of Massachusetts by Martin Johnson Heade," *American Art Journal* 27 (1995-96), pp. 84-98.

7. John Wilmerding, *American Marine Painting*, 2d ed. (New York: Harry N. Abrams, 1987), pp. 124-125.

8. See Sarah Cash, *Ominous Hush: The Thunderstorm Paintings of Martin Johnson Heade*, exh. cat. (Fort Worth, Tex.: Amon Carter Museum, 1994), pp. 130-131.

9. For a discussion of different readings of this work, see Stebbins, "Picturing Heade," in this catalogue. J. Gray Sweeney writes about the painting in "A 'very peculiar' Picture: Martin Johnson Heade's *Thunderstorm over Narragansett Bay*," *Archives of American Art Journal* 28, no. 4 (1988), pp. 2-14.

10. T. C. Grannis, *National Academy of Design: Exhibition of 1868* (New York: D. Appleton & Company, 1868), p. 87; "The Art Association: Third Day of the Exhibition — More of the Pictures," *Brooklyn Daily Eagle*, March 21, 1868, p. 2; "National Academy of Design, Forty-third Annual Exhibition: Fifth Notice," *New York Leader*, May 16, 1868, p. 5.

11. Heade did make one last coastal thunderstorm, an oil sketch on paper, *Thunderstorm at the Shore*, about 1870-71, $9^{5}/_{8}$ x $18^{1}/_{2}$ in., Carnegie Museum of Art, Pittsburgh.

12. *Becalmed* is inscribed on the verso, "Off the Thimble Islands."

I

APPROACHING THUNDER STORM, *1859*

The Metropolitan Museum of Art

2

SEASCAPE: SUNRISE, *1860*

Private Collection

3

SEASCAPE: SUNSET, *1861*

The Detroit Institute of Arts

4

APPROACHING STORM: BEACH NEAR NEWPORT, *about 1861–63*

Museum of Fine Arts, Boston

5

DAWN, *1862*

Museum of Fine Arts, Boston

6

TWILIGHT, SINGING BEACH, *1863*

Fine Arts Museums of San Francisco

7

THE STRANDED BOAT, *1863*

Museum of Fine Arts, Boston

8

THUNDER STORM ON NARRAGANSETT BAY, *1868*

Amon Carter Museum, Fort Worth, Texas

9

BECALMED, LONG ISLAND SOUND, *1876*

Theodore G. and Eleanor S. Congdon

MARSHES

TODAY WE KNOW OF more than 120 views of the northeastern salt marsh by Heade, accounting for nearly one-fifth of his entire oeuvre. Clement and Hutton in 1884 accurately concluded that "he painted more of them than of any other class of subjects."[1] Heade had begun to paint the marsh by 1859, for a Boston critic in December of that year admired his "meadow scene in Newburyport, taken at sunset . . . [with a] stream that runs through the meadow."[2] Heade continued to work with the marsh theme until his death, forty-five years later. His favorite marshes were the ones in the adjoining towns of Newbury and Newburyport in the northeastern corner of Massachusetts, but he also painted them at Rowley, Lynn, and Marshfield in the same state, as well as in Connecticut and Long Island. In addition, after he moved back to New York in 1866 he painted numerous views of the Hoboken meadows in New Jersey. The marsh views are typically smaller in size (only rarely exceeding 15 x 30 in.) and are even more insistently horizontal in shape than the marine subjects that Heade was also painting during the 1860s and 1870s. They are warmer, more approachable pictures than the seascapes. Where the latter feature stark contrasts of sea and sky, or the powerful, irregular forms of rocks, waves, or violent storms, the marsh scenes depict the slower rhythms of nature and the men and boys who rake the hay, hunt and fish, or simply walk there. They have a domestic quality, in both their size and sub-ject matter. Heade's marsh scenes, like his marines, orchids, and other subjects, seem very much to make up a series, rather than being examples of duplication, for there are pentimenti and alterations — showing the artist adjusting the haystacks and other elements — in nearly every one of them. If the exotic orchids represented for Heade the embodiment of the tropics, then the marshes became his quintessential landscape subject.

Why paint the marsh? First, Heade demanded of himself originality, and, though the marsh was familiar and ubiquitous, it was a new subject for the American painter. Equally important, the marsh was simply a place Heade loved: on the one hand it represented untouched nature — an ideal place for hunting and fishing — and on the other it was a natural farmland, where hay was harvested and stacked. If Heade was an intermediary figure between the Hudson River School and the next generation, then too the marsh might be seen as an intermediate landscape that lies somewhere between wilderness and the pastoral.

The chronology of Heade's marshes is difficult to ascertain, because only a very few of them are dated. Having taken up the subject in 1858 or 1859, the painter had mastered the subtle depiction of the greens of the marsh and the grays of an overcast day no later than 1861, as one sees in *Cloudy Day, Rhode Island* (Museum of Fine Arts, Boston), of that year. Two

Cat. 14 (detail)

years later, in 1863, he executed the atypically large *Sunrise on the Marshes* (cat. 12), which is also unusual in the relatively sizeable fisherman and boy in the right foreground. Many of Heade's marsh scenes in the years up to 1863 are experimental in nature, and the most fully developed marshes with imminent storms appear to date after his return from his extensive travels of 1863-66. *Summer Showers* at the Brooklyn Museum of Art (cat. 10) depicts the Newburyport marsh under threatening conditions, with a band of dark clouds across the top of the canvas suggesting the approach of rain. *Sudden Shower, Newbury Marshes* at Yale (cat. 13) — a companion work of exactly the same dimensions — shows the same marsh in a slightly more developed composition, for now one sees the whole of the meandering river in the form of a double S-curve as it recedes into the distance. Showers fall in the foreground, while warm sunlight has broken through the clouds to bathe the distance, where farmers rake the hay. The huge haystacks themselves echo the course of the river as they perform a stately, measured march toward the horizon. A third work in the series, at the Butler Institute (cat. 14), is equally successful. Moving elsewhere in the marsh to a wider river, Heade reverses his formula, now painting the foreground and one huge haystack in bright sunlight while showers pour down in the distance under one of his most brilliantly painted skies. Scholars have wondered where Heade could possibly have learned to paint the stormy skies he did in this work, in *Thunder Storm on Narragansett Bay*, and elsewhere, for there is almost nothing like them in Hudson River School painting. Some scholars have suggested the possible influence of the French artist Gustave Courbet, whose renderings of showers Heade might have seen in London in 1864-65, but this fails to account for his competent handling of stormy and hazy weather in the years before this trip. While no other American specialized in depicting these conditions, there were any number of painters including James Suydam and George Inness whose work Heade would have known, and who might have affected his approach.

As John Wilmerding has written, "the marsh is the one landscape in constant flux,"[3] owing to the fact that its rivers are tidal. Interestingly, Heade almost always painted the marsh rivers at high tide, just as his seashore views frequently depict low tide. The farmers' haying "season" had its own regular schedule, because the cutting and stacking of this natural crop could only be done when the tides were running unusually low and the grass was dry. And as John I. H. Baur commented, Heade was especially sensitive to "the play of sunlight and cloud shadows on salt marshes, the subtly changing tones of mist or the gradations of color in a sunset."[4] For this painter, the sky and clouds, the alternation of showers and sunlight, the sense of movement and change, all echo the rhythms of man and nature below. *Newburyport Meadows* at the Metropolitan Museum (cat. 11) shows rays of sunlight just as they break through a gray sky; water is seen here only in puddles, and the emphasis on the sky is greater than in earlier marshes. Quite different is *Marshfield Meadows* (cat. 18), where one follows the winding river and the receding haystacks up to the barrier dunes, beyond which breaking waves are visible. Though there are failures in the series, particularly among the sunsets and the New Jersey scenes, there are also superb examples from throughout the late 1860s and 1870s. Among the later examples, San Francisco's mistitled *Great Swamp* (cat. 15) depicts a northeastern marsh in a fog at flood tide and is one of the most evocative and atmospheric of all of the series. *Two Fishermen in the Marsh, at Sunset* (cat. 17) is another picture which includes a man and boy, presumably a father and son, a favorite device of Heade's. In this work the whole landscape resonates with the pink glow of the setting sun, and both the coloration and relatively loose brushwork recall Heade's orchid pictures of the same mid-1870s period. Finally, another work of the seventies is the extraordinary *Hayfields: A Clear Day* (cat. 19), one of the strongest of the series with the cumulus clouds gathered at the horizon, the lengthening shadows of late afternoon, and the pattern of shade and sunlight across the marsh grasses.

THEODORE E. STEBBINS, JR.

NOTES

1. Clara Erskine Clement and Laurence Hutton, *Artists of the Nineteenth Century and Their Work* (Boston and New York: Houghton, Mifflin and Company, 1884), vol. 1, p. 340.

2. "Art Items," *Boston Transcript*, December 1, 1859, p. 2.

3. John Wilmerding, in *Master Paintings from the Butler Institute of American Art*, ed. Irene S. Sweetkind (New York: Harry N. Abrams, in association with the Butler Institute of American Art, 1994), p. 113.

4. John I. H. Baur, "Trends in American Painting, 1815-1865," *M. and M. Karolik Collection of American Paintings, 1815–1865* (Cambridge, Mass.: Harvard University Press, 1949), p. xliii.

10

SUMMER SHOWERS, *about 1866–76*

Brooklyn Museum of Art

II

NEWBURYPORT MEADOWS, *about 1871–75*

The Metropolitan Museum of Art

12

The Flint Institute of Arts, Flint, Michigan

13

SUDDEN SHOWER, NEWBURY MARSHES, *about 1866–76*

Yale University Art Gallery

14

SALT MARSH HAY, *about 1866–76*

The Butler Institute of American Art, Youngstown, Ohio

15

16

SUNSET MARSH (SINKING SUN), *1868*

David L. Long and Elizabeth Valk Long

17

TWO FISHERMEN IN THE MARSH, AT SUNSET, *about 1876–82*

Private Collection

18

MARSHFIELD MEADOWS, *about 1877–78*

The Currier Gallery of Art, Manchester, New Hampshire

19

HAYFIELDS: A CLEAR DAY, *about 1871–80*

Jo Ann and Julian Ganz, Jr.

*A*BOUT ONE QUARTER of Heade's landscapes represent inland views — mountains, lakes, and valleys — in the traditional compositional formats we associate with the Hudson River School. Into this category of works that look conventional at first sight, however, fall a number of Heade's boldest and most experimental paintings.

Lake George (cat. 20), for example, depicts one of the most popular subjects of the landscape painters in a manner that illustrates how far Heade actually was — in style and in practice — from the mainstream of the school. Between 1857 and 1862 Heade took several summer sketching trips to the White Mountains, the coast of Maine, the Thousand Islands, New Brunswick, and Lake Champlain. While working at Champlain in 1860 or 1862 he must have gone a few miles south to the more mountainous and scenic Lake George, which had been the subject of a poem by Thomas Cole and of numerous paintings by John F. Kensett, John W. Casilear, and other New York painters. For Kensett and those who followed, Lake George represented the quintessential Adirondack scene: cool, clear waters surrounded by rocky ledges, islands covered with virgin fir, picturesque mountains rising from the water's edge, with just a trace of man's presence. Heade's picture ignores this convention. First, he rejected the favored view toward the Narrows and instead took a vantage point looking north from Silver Bay on the west side of the lake, from which one sees none of the lake's distinguishing features. Equally important, Heade did not employ the cool greens and grays that Kensett and others favored but instead used hues that are "hot and dry," as Diana Strazdes suggests;[1] Heade's colors — warm tans, pinks, grays, and pale greens — are those of the arid desert rather than the lush Adirondacks. Finally, he placed much of his emphasis on the painting's foreground, which occupies the lower third of the composition. At the left, a man launches his rowboat, straining to push it off the beach, while at right, a flat, rocky ledge is delineated with scintillating high-Ruskinian detail. In this area and across the whole, quiet composition, Heade adopted the style of the British Pre-Raphaelite landscapists. He had likely seen the important *Exhibition of British Art* that had been shown in Philadelphia, New York, and Boston in 1857–58 and would have found prototypes for his *Lake George* in such works as John Brett's *Glacier of Rosenlaui* (The Tate Gallery, London) and in others by John Ruskin, Edward Lear, and Ford Madox Brown.[2] In addition, as Annette Blaugrund has suggested, he might well have learned about the highly detailed technique from one of his neighbors in the Tenth Street Studio Building, the American Pre-Raphaelite Charles H. Moore.[3] In any case, *Lake George* is unique as Heade's only large-scale foray in the Ruskinian style.[4]

Similarly, in 1868 Heade employed a traditional hills-and-valley composition to conduct another, less explicable experiment. The painting long known as *Spring Shower, Connecticut Valley* is one Heade had entitled *April Showers* (cat. 21); it was described by a New York reviewer in October 1868 as "a large picture, giving a broad open valley . . . running up and back to the hills in the distance. A little bit of water is in the right foreground. In the right background the hill-tops are enveloped in black, angry clouds."[5] The writer goes on to admire "the bright, rich colors of the apple blossoms in the front middle ground," confirming the identification of the work. It is difficult to imagine a work more different from *Thunder Storm on Narragansett Bay*, with its harsh, contrasting palette of lights and darks and its super-realism, which was executed in the same year. In *April Showers*, Heade employed a feathery, stippled touch, giving only the distant hills any real substance. The range of hues is narrow, with grays and greens predominating, and value contrasts were similarly restricted, from relatively high-keyed pinks and yellow-greens on the foreground trees to the medium greens and grays of the hills and sky. Color and brushwork hide the details, so that one can easily overlook the stone wall and its wooden gate in the foreground, or the covered haystack and farmhouse in the middle ground.

The subjects of this painting are color and light, momentary change in the weather, and the passing effects of a shower, all of which were preoccupations for Heade, and he described them in numerous marsh scenes and other works. But here he has loosened his brushwork to a remarkable degree, and one cannot help thinking of *April Showers* as an extraordinary precursor to the impressionist style. Yet even though the painting was much admired by contemporary critics, Heade made no attempts to follow up on it until 1874, when he made a series of four or five related works. Either he was unsatisfied with these paintings or they failed to sell, for he never again returned to the subject of the flowering apple tree or to anything like a nascent impressionist style.

THEODORE E. STEBBINS, JR.

NOTES

1. Diana J. Strazdes, "Lake George," in *American Paradise: The World of the Hudson River School*, exh. cat. (New York: The Metropolitan Museum of Art, 1988), p. 167.

2. See Susan P. Casteras, "The 1857–58 Exhibition of English Art in America: Critical Responses to Pre-Raphaelitism," in Linda S. Ferber and William H. Gerdts, *The New Path: Ruskin and the American Pre-Raphaelites*, exh. cat. (Brooklyn: The Brooklyn Museum, 1985), pp. 109–133.

3. Annette Blaugrund, "Lake George," in *The New Path*, p. 267.

4. Both *Dawn*, 1862 (cat. 5), and *The Lookout, Burlington, Vermont* (unlocated), about 1862, demonstrate the Ruskinian style on a smaller scale.

5. "Fine Arts. What the Artists Are Doing. M. J. Heade," *New York Evening Post*, October 13, 1868, p. 1.

Overleaf: Cat. 20 (detail)

20

LAKE GEORGE, *1862*

Museum of Fine Arts, Boston

21

APRIL SHOWERS, *1868*

Museum of Fine Arts, Boston

TROPICAL LANDSCAPES

*I*NSPIRED NO DOUBT by his friend Frederic E. Church and by the success of Church's picture *The Heart of the Andes* (The Metropolitan Museum of Art, New York), which had electrified the public in 1859, Heade undertook three trips to Latin America between 1863 and 1870. However, unlike Church, who followed in the footsteps of the great naturalist Alexander von Humboldt to Colombia and Ecuador, Heade decided to visit Brazil for his first Latin American journey.[1] The *Boston Transcript* reported in August 1863, "M. J. Heade . . . is about to visit Brazil, to paint those winged jewels, the hummingbirds." Heade must have been encouraged to select Brazil as his destination by another friend, the Reverend James Cooley Fletcher, acting secretary of the United States legation at Rio de Janeiro in the 1850s and author with the Reverend D. P. Kidder of *Brazil and the Brazilians* in 1857, in which it was noted, "Everywhere throughout Brazil this little winged gem, in many varieties, abounds."[2] Sailing from New York on the *Golden City* on September 2, 1863, Heade arrived in Rio de Janeiro on September 20.

Although Heade's primary objective was to study and paint the hummingbirds, he also produced a few landscapes during his six-month sojourn, including several views of Rio de Janeiro Bay.[3] However, he apparently began to work seriously on landscape only after the group of hummingbird pictures had been completed. On January 10, 1864, he had an interview with Emperor Dom Pedro II, to whom Heade had been introduced by the Reverend Fletcher,[4] during which the emperor encouraged him to paint Brazilian scenery and even recommended an ideal vantage point for a view of the harbor at Rio. On January 17 Heade wrote in his journal, "I went up on Boa Viagem to-day; from which the emperor told me I should take a sketch of the city. The view is certainly one of the most beautiful that I remember ever to have seen. It is a little fortified hill . . . from the top . . . there is nothing to intercept the view in any direction, and the panorama is glorious."[5]

It was probably from Boa Viagem or the nearby district of São Domingos in the city of Niteroy on the eastern side of the bay across from Rio de Janeiro that Heade painted *Sunset: Harbor at Rio* (cat. 23). Heade accurately depicted the dramatic mountains that encircle the bay: from the left, Gavea (or Table Mountain); the tall, uniquely shaped Mount Corcovado, which Heade had climbed; and to the right the Tijuca Mountains. In the foreground a banana tree reinforces the tropical character of the painting,[6] and behind it the steam vessels and sailboats indicate by their scale the great size of the harbor, as do the tiny buildings of Rio on the opposite shore.

While *Sunset: Harbor at Rio* is topographically accurate, *Brazilian Forest* (cat. 22) is an evocation of the South American rain forest rather than a precise rendering of an actual scene. Heade painted *Brazilian Forest* in London in 1864 and inscribed on the stretcher: "From Forest Studies in South America — The Tree Fern." Obviously captivated by this exotic plant, Heade made the carefully painted tree fern the centerpiece of his composition. By choosing a vertical orientation for the canvas and a low point of view, Heade brings the viewer to the edge of the inaccessible, dank, tree-tangled rain forest. Professor Louis Agassiz, the great naturalist from Harvard College, and his wife, Elizabeth Cary Agassiz, a founder and president of Radcliffe College, who visited Brazil the year after Heade, described the Brazilian forest:

the impenetrability of the mass here . . . makes the density, darkness, and solemnity of the woods so impressive. It seems as if the mode of growth — many of the trees shooting up to an immense height, but branching only toward the top — were meant to give room to the legion of parasites, sipos, lianas, and climbing plants of all kinds which fill the intervening spaces. . . . The tree-ferns . . . are . . . modern representatives of past types.[7]

Behind the tree fern, Heade painted a dark pool of water, flowing out near the bottom of the picture, and to the right the small figure of a crouching hunter with a gun and a dog. Heade was an avid sportsman and had a reputation for being an excellent shot; he included hunters in a number of pictures of northern salt marshes, but this is the only tropical scene with such a figure.[8]

Heade must have been pleased with this work because he entered it in an exhibition at the British Institution in London in 1865 with a price of sixty pounds. Although it did not sell in London, it was purchased on Heade's return, in 1866, by Governor Henry Lippitt of Rhode Island, who also bought *The Harbor at Rio de Janeiro* (1864, Mr. and Mrs. Stuart P. Feld) and *Two Hummingbirds with Their Young* (cat. 51). Heade also entered *Brazilian Forest* in the National Academy of Design exhibition in 1866, and Lippitt was listed as its owner.

In a third major tropical painting, *View from Fern-Tree Walk, Jamaica* (cat. 24), Heade looks from a dense jungle onto a sunlit bay. Painted seventeen years after Heade's third and final trip to Latin America in 1870, *View from Fern-Tree Walk, Jamaica* was commissioned by Henry Morrison Flagler, John D. Rockefeller's partner in the Standard Oil Company and later the developer of Florida into "America's Riviera." As Flagler's grand Ponce de Leon Hotel in St. Augustine neared completion, Heade wrote to his friend Eben J. Loomis, "I'm painting two landscapes for him (8 ft. long) which will take some thousands out of his pocket, but I think he can stand it." In another letter to Loomis, Heade wrote, "My two big pictures, for the parlor of the big hotel, are nearly completed. One is a Jamaica picture, with tree ferns & things, & I think its a pretty neat thing — for me. The other is a Florida scene, a Sun-Set."[9] These two pictures, *View from Fern-Tree Walk, Jamaica* and *The Great Florida Sunset* (fig. 44) are the two largest of Heade's paintings.

View from Fern-Tree Walk follows the compositional format Heade employed in his 1874 painting *Coast of Jamaica* (fig. 13) and was based on both the painter's sketches and his memory. When he visited Jamaica in 1870, he had made several pencil studies (figs. 9 and 10) of the dense vegetation, which he used primarily for the left side of the picture. Heade could have heard of Fern Walk from Church, who had sketched it on his own Jamaican trip of 1865. James H. Stark, in his *History and Guide to Jamaica*, wrote of the four-mile-long Fern Gully:

The scenery through this ravine is unique, and can be surpassed by few other places in the world. It is from forty to fifty feet in width, just wide enough for a good road; the sides rise perpendicular to a height of hundreds of feet; only the noonday sun penetrates to the road. The steep rocks on each side are literally covered with the loveliest of ferns, which grow in the richest profusion. Tree-ferns of magnificent proportions, as well as the tiniest and most delicate specimens, are seen. The forest trees, too, are laden with orchids and with long creepers, which descend from the branches thirty feet or more to the surface below.[10]

Heade must have decided to contrast the dense forest as described here with an open vista of a serene bay. In the foreground he carefully delineated the tropical vegetation, including the philodendron plants with arrow-shaped leaves in the left foreground (also visible in fig. 10), an aloe plant in the right foreground, and several spectacular tree ferns in patches of sunlight. In the middle ground one can see a tiny figure leading cattle up the path. Threatening clouds overhead with fair-weather clouds in the distance indicate changeable weather conditions.

Although Heade probably started to study South American scenery to use as settings for his hummingbird pictures, he soon found the landscape of interest for its own sake. The numerous studies of tropical vegetation he had made with the eye of a naturalist during his three trips would serve him for many years while he produced paintings for an American public fascinated with exotic scenes from its own hemisphere.

JANET L. COMEY

Fig. 9. *The Jamaica Sketchbook: "Fern Tree Walk/Jamaica,"* about 1870, graphite on paper. Museum of Fine Arts, Boston, Gift of Richard and Susanna Nash, 1997.297.

Fig. 10. *Large Karolik Sketchbook: Sketches of Tropical Vegetation*, about 1866, graphite on paper. Museum of Fine Arts, Boston, Bequest of Maxim Karolik.

NOTES

1. See Katherine Emma Manthorne, *Tropical Renaissance: North American Artists Exploring Latin America, 1839–1879* (Washington, D.C., and London: Smithsonian Institution Press, 1989).

2. The Reverend James C. Fletcher and the Reverend D. P. Kidder, D.D., *Brazil and the Brazilians* (Boston: Little, Brown, and Company, 1867), p. 484.

3. Heade's other paintings of Rio de Janeiro Bay include *The Harbor at Rio de Janeiro*, 1864 (Mr. and Mrs. Stuart P. Feld), and *Seascape (Brazilian View)*, 1865 (Spanierman Gallery, New York), both painted from approximately the same vantage point as cat. 23; *Rio de Janeiro Bay*, 1864 (fig. 21), *Coast of Brazil*, 1864 (Alexander Gallery, New York), *Harbor in Brazil*, 1865 (C. Vaughan Goodman), and *Harbor Scene, Rio de Janeiro*, 1865 (private collection), all painted from another vantage point in the bay.

4. Martin Johnson Heade, "Brazil/London Journal," manuscript, Museum of Fine Arts, Boston, Gift of Richard and Susanna Nash, 1997.296, p. 27. Heade wrote that the emperor "wishes to know whether I had yet painted any landscapes, and I had to answer that I had not, but that I was engaged on a picture of Rio. He said I ought to take my picture from Boa Viagem, as the view from that fortification was very beautiful."

5. Ibid., p. 29.

6. I am grateful to Dr. Gustavo A. Romero, Keeper, Oakes Ames Orchid Herbarium, Harvard University, for his help in identifying plants in these paintings.

7. Professor Louis Agassiz and Mrs. Louis Agassiz, *A Journey in Brazil* (Boston and New York: Houghton, Mifflin and Company, 1891), p. 109.

8. Other paintings with hunters are *Two Hunters in a Landscape* (Fundación Colección Thyssen-Bornemisza, Madrid), *Hunters Resting* (fig. 34), *Duck Hunters in a Twilight Marsh* (private collection), and *Marsh with a Hunter* (private collection).

9. April 11 and June 16, 1887, letters, Martin Johnson Heade to Eben J. Loomis, Loomis-Wilder Family Papers, Manuscripts and Archives, Yale University Library. Before the Loomis-Heade correspondence was discovered, scholars had surmised that *View from Fern-Tree Walk, Jamaica* was the work that Heade had exhibited in the 1870s under the title *Jamaica* but that remained unsold until Flagler bought it in 1887, whereupon Heade signed and dated it. See Stebbins, *The Life and Works of Martin Johnson Heade* (New Haven, Conn.: Yale University Press, 1975), p. 94.

10. James H. Stark, *Stark's Jamaica Guide* (Boston: James H. Stark, Publisher, 1898), p. 133.

22

23

SUNSET: HARBOR AT RIO, *1864*

The Museum of American Art of the Pennsylvania Academy of the Fine Arts, Philadelphia

24

VIEW FROM FERN-TREE WALK, JAMAICA, *1887*

Manoogian Collection

*H*EADE began to paint floral still lifes in about 1860, producing nearly 150 of them over the next forty years. He rarely painted fruit, except to add an orange to an orange blossom painting or a passion fruit to one of the *Gems*, and although he was an ardent sportsman, he never painted dead game. He loved flowers; as he wrote in his Brazil/London journal, "it is a task imposed on me — principally self imposed, but by custom grown into a sort of duty — to gather and 'fix' a beautiful bouquet for the breakfast table; and we often indulge in two or three."[1] Heade's still lifes typically have a highly realistic look, as if the artist had just gathered and "fixed" the bouquets.

One of Heade's earliest dated still lifes, *Trailing Arbutus*, 1860 (cat. 25), is one of two known paintings of that flower.[2] Heade emphasized the low, creeping nature of this evergreen plant by using the horizontal orientation of the canvas. He arranged the trailing arbutus, which grows in the woods of Canada and the northern United States, in a brown vase on a plain table to make a pleasing, low, triangular composition, and he realistically depicted the blemished leaves and the occasional dying blossom. The solitary acorn recalls the forest habitat of the plant. The correspondent for the *Crayon*, perhaps referring to this work, wrote, "Mr. Heade, of Providence, gives us occasional glimpses of flowers and trailing vines — such exquisite groups — that we are almost tempted to wish that he were less successful as a landscapist."[3]

In *Roses and Heliotrope in a Vase on a Marble Tabletop*, 1862 (cat. 26), Heade portrayed two of his favorite flowers; he included the purple heliotrope in some fifteen of his works and roses in over eighty-five later paintings. The rose here may be the Safrano, a tea rose introduced in 1839.[4] Popular in southern gardens, tea roses have a tendency to nod as if the blooms were too big for their stems. Here Heade employed a simple vase, probably of tinted Parian ware, whose curvilinear shape and color complement the roses, and placed it on a marble table, introducing a bit of drapery and a sprig of heliotrope to frame the vase. A gentle light flowing in from the left helps to model the forms. Just as he had chosen the plain brown table and acorn as suitable accompaniments for the woodland trailing arbutus, here Heade selected a marble table and drapery as appropriate trappings for the more elegant roses and heliotrope.

A Vase of Corn Lilies and Heliotrope, 1863 (cat. 27), seems a paean to early summer in America with its red, white, and blue hues, in the strawberries still on the vine, and in the ordinary fringed shawl draped on the plain table. Commenting on the naturalism of Heade's painting, Ella Foshay has written, "Heade seems to have plucked his live specimens and reordered them in a vase set before his easel, since heliotropes and corn lilies grow wild (and can be cultivated) in the north-eastern United States and come into bloom during the same season, from May to August."[5] Here Heade made the frosted glass vase less prominent and gently illuminated the flowers, strawberries, and drapery.

Some of Heade's most effective flower pictures are those with a single spectacular blossom, as in *Red Flower in a Vase* (cat. 30). Here the blown glass vase holds a splendid double crinum lily, accompanied by acacia and a moss rosebud on the table. The drama of the painting is enhanced by the black velvet drapery with its gold fringe echoing the yellow stamens of the lily, and the gold box adds further luxuriance. *The White Rose*, about 1874–80 (cat. 34), depicts a large white tea rose, possibly *Devoniensis*, or magnolia rose. Although it includes on the table a red Général Jacqueminot rose (one of Heade's favorites) along with a pink rosebud in a vase, the focus of the composition is the large white blossom. The oversized, forbidding quality of this blossom recalls Heade's orchids and his later passion flowers and suggests how different his intentions were in comparison to other rose painters of his day, such as George C. Lambdin.

By the late 1860s Heade had abandoned the simple background and provided more ornate settings for his arrangements. In *Vase of Mixed Flowers*, about 1872 (cat. 29), the patterns on the wall, table covering, and drapery as well as the elaborate vase threaten to overwhelm the bouquet. Yet the wall and table coverings are muted, and the colors of the materials complement rather than distract from the blooms in the vase. This may be the painting to which the "Art Notes" column of the *New York Evening Post* referred in October 1872: "M. J. Heade has just finished an exquisite flower subject — a group of flowers in a vase with rich drapery surrounding it. The group

is composed of rare varieties of roses, carnations, orange blossoms, heather plant and azaleas. The picture is at present on view in Mr. Heade's studio." The painting was purchased by William Barnes Bement, a Philadelphia manufacturer and inventor of machine tools and director of the Pennsylvania Academy of the Fine Arts from 1874 to 1897. In an 1884 catalogue of Bement's collection, Charles M. Skinner wrote, "Mr. Heade contributes so little to exhibitions nowadays that the younger generation does not know, or has forgotten, his flowers, his humming-birds, his tropic landscapes, and his sunsets. . . . This illustration of his work shows him at his best. It is a dainty vase filled with freshly-gathered flowers, arranged without stiffness, and painted with conscientious fidelity to nature."[6]

Although Heade favored the rose above all other flowers, he was also partial to the apple blossom. He painted some twenty-five still lifes of apple blossoms as well as several landscapes of apple trees (see cat. 21). His earliest depiction of apple blossoms was probably in 1865 in *Ruby Throat of North America* (cat. 53). In 1867 Heade painted his earliest still lifes of apple blossoms, including *Apple Blossoms in a Vase* (private collection) and *Branch of Apple Blossoms against a Cloudy Sky* (cat. 31).

In *A Spray of Apple Blossoms*, 1870 (cat. 32), Heade depicted the branch against a plain background, a composition that Bruce Weber notes appears to derive its "arrangement from botanical illustrations."[7] In 1871 a correspondent for the *New York Evening Post* wrote, "M. J. Heade is painting among other flower subjects, a study of apple blossoms, with humming birds perched upon the branches among them . . . he is devoting the most careful attention to its elaboration and finish."[8] The critic may well have been referring to *Apple Blossoms and*

Hummingbird, 1871 (cat. 33). Here Heade used a similar format to that he was employing for the orchid-and-hummingbird series he began in 1871, focusing on the ruby-throated hummingbird and apple blossom branch in the foreground, as if seen through a telescope, with the rest of the apple orchard in the distance.

The critic Henry Tuckerman captured the essence of Heade's apple blossom still lifes when he wrote, "Mr. Heade embodied the very soul of vernal bloom and tenderness in two or three modest, lovely pictures of 'Apple Blossoms;' we could not have believed so simple and common an object could be made so suggestive; but they give the very key-note of the season; they sweetly hint, not only an orchard, but a landscape; we seem to inhale their odor, and see their pink and white flakes quiver in the breeze of May down on the newly sprung grass."[9]

JANET L. COMEY

NOTES

1. "Brazil/London Journal," November 29, 1863, manuscript, Museum of Fine Arts, Boston, Gift of Richard and Susanna Nash, 1997.296, p. 17.

2. The other painting of trailing arbutus, presently unlocated, was the original picture from which the chromolithograph *Flowers of Hope* was made by L. Prang & Co. of Boston in 1870. The print sold for $5.00 and was a companion piece to *Flowers of Memory* by Elizabeth Remington. Heade made a drawing of a trailing arbutus leaf in one of his sketchbooks, noting "natural size." *Jamaica Sketchbook*, Museum of Fine Arts, Boston, Gift of Richard and Susanna Nash, 1997.297.

3. "Domestic Art Gossip," *Crayon* 7, pt. 9 (September 1860), p. 264.

4. I am grateful to Stephen Scaniello of the Brooklyn Botanic Garden for his help in identifying the roses in Heade's paintings and to Dorothy-Lee Jones of the Jones Museum of Glass and Ceramics, Sebago, Maine, for her assistance with the vases.

5. Ella M. Foshay, *Reflections of Nature: Flowers in American Art,* exh. cat. (New York: Whitney Museum of American Art, 1984), p. 52.

6. Charles M. Skinner, *Catalogue of Works of Art of William B. Bement of Philadelphia, Pa.* (Philadelphia: Press of J. B. Lippincott, 1884), unpaginated.

7. Bruce Weber, *The Apple of America: The Apple in Nineteenth-Century American Art*, exh. cat. (New York: Berry-Hill Galleries, 1993), p. 11.

8. "Art Notes," *New York Evening Post*, March 30, 1871, p. 2.

9. Henry T. Tuckerman, *Book of the Artists: American Artist Life* (New York: G. P. Putnam & Son, 1867), p. 543.

25

TRAILING ARBUTUS, *1860*

Mr. and Mrs. Stuart P. Feld

26

ROSES AND HELIOTROPE IN A VASE ON A MARBLE TABLETOP, *1862*

Private Collection

27

A VASE OF CORN LILIES AND HELIOTROPE, *1863*

The Saint Louis Art Museum

28

WILDFLOWERS IN A BROWN VASE, *about 1860–65*

Philadelphia Museum of Art

29

VASE OF MIXED FLOWERS, *about 1872*

Museum of Fine Arts, Boston

30

31

BRANCH OF APPLE BLOSSOMS AGAINST A CLOUDY SKY, *1867*

Private Collection

32

A SPRAY OF APPLE BLOSSOMS, *1870*

Mr. and Mrs. Henry Luce III

33

APPLE BLOSSOMS AND HUMMINGBIRD, *1871*

Addison Gallery of American Art, Phillips Academy, Andover, Massachusetts

34

THE WHITE ROSE, *about 1874–80*

James and Barbara Palmer

THE GEMS OF BRAZIL

On AUGUST 12, 1863, a notice in the *Boston Transcript* reported Heade's plan to visit Brazil to paint its hummingbirds, explaining, "It is his intention in Brazil to depict the richest and most brilliant of the hummingbird family, —about which he is so great an enthusiast— to prepare in London or Paris a large and elegant Album on these wonderful little creatures, got up in the highest style of art. He is only fulfilling the dream of his boyhood in doing so." Heade was likely inspired to undertake this project by the publications of John James Audubon and John Gould. He was familiar with Audubon's four-volume *Birds of America*, which included plates after Audubon's watercolors engraved and hand-colored in London between 1827 and 1838. John Gould had published a five-volume monograph on hummingbirds between 1849 and 1861, comprising 360 plates of hand-colored lithographs. Gould drew his hummingbirds in England entirely from specimens, and Heade may have thought that he could improve on Gould's work by observing and portraying the birds in their native environment. Years later in an article in *Forest and Stream*, Heade contrasted himself with Gould, writing, "His great work on the hummingbirds of South America was not made up from personal knowledge of their character and habits, but gathered from travelers and explorers. He never set his foot on South American soil, the habitat of this large family of birds."[1]

Found only in the New World, the hummingbird has fascinated travelers since Columbus. Since there is only one species (ruby-throated hummingbird) native to the region east of the Rocky Mountains in North America, it was natural that Heade —a self-described "monomaniac" about hummingbirds— was drawn to Brazil, where a multitude of species can be found. Because of their iridescent feathers, hummingbirds are often collectively referred to as "gems" or "jewels," and many of their specific names invoke precious stones (ruby, topaz, amethyst) or indicate the enchantment associated with these smallest members of the bird family (fairy, coquette, woodnymph).

Arriving in Rio de Janeiro on September 20, 1863, Heade must have begun painting the hummingbirds almost immediately, because he recorded in his journal on October 25 the comments made by Brazil's Emperor Dom Pedro II on seeing his work: "He expressed great delight on seeing two of my unfinished oiseau mouche . . . and desired me to revisit the palace when they were all completed."[2] Heade found Brazil ideal for the naturalist: "There is probably no country where a person interested in ornithology, entomology, botany, mineralogy or beautiful scenery could find so much to keep him entertained."[3] Not only did he sketch the hummingbirds, but he also studied their diet and nesting habits. In his 1892 letter to *Forest and Stream* discussing hummingbirds, he wrote,

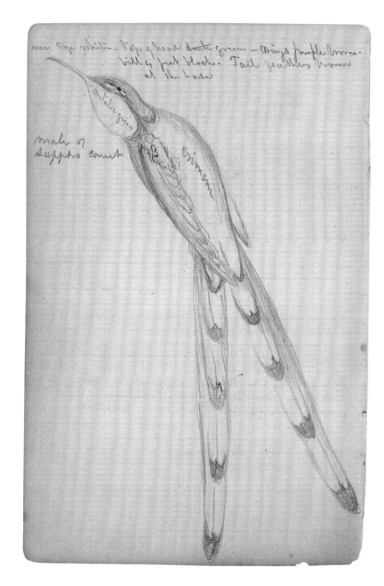

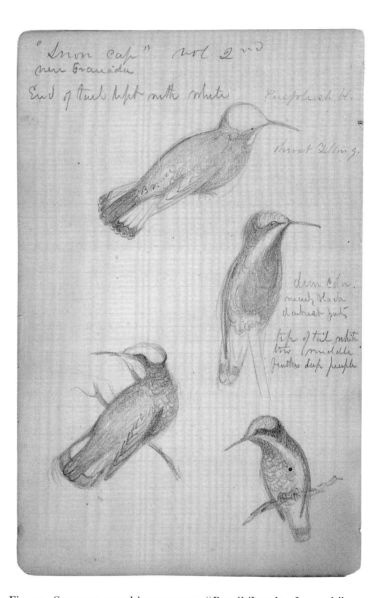

Fig. 11. *Sappho Comet*, graphite on paper, "Brazil/London Journal," 1863–65. Museum of Fine Arts, Boston, Gift of Richard and Susanna Nash, 1997.296.

Fig. 12. *Snowcap*, graphite on paper, "Brazil/London Journal," 1863–65. Museum of Fine Arts, Boston, Gift of Richard and Susanna Nash, 1996.296.

"I dissected one in South America and washed out the crop in a basin of water, when scores of minute insects floated through it."[4] While in Rio de Janeiro, a trading center for skins of birds from all over South America, Heade also collected specimens of both Brazilian and non-Brazilian species.

On January 11, 1864, Heade, still in Brazil, wrote that although he had received offers to buy his paintings, "as to the birds, an offer of 10,000 dollars would be no inducement to sell them." By then he was in touch with M. & N. Hanhart, a leading lithographic printing firm in London, noting that he had already sent two pictures from Brazil to Hanhart to be lithographed.[5] On February 14, 1864, Heade exhibited twelve paintings of hummingbirds at the Exposição Geral das Bellas Artes (Universal Exposition of the Fine Arts) in Rio de Janeiro, which were listed in the catalogue as "Gems of Brazil — a part of the collection of 20 canvases, which will be chromo-lithographed and published in London. Work dedicated to His Imperial Majesty Dom Pedro II."[6] On March 30, 1864, Dom Pedro, delighted with Heade's distinguished works in this exhibition, named him a Knight of the Order of the Rose.[7]

Heade left Brazil on April 8 and arrived in London on May 5 to work on the book. During the next several months Heade studied the ornithological works of Gould, Alexander Wilson, and George Shaw, as well as George Robert Gray's *Genera of Birds* (1849) and Philip Henry Gosse's *Birds of Jamaica* (1847). His journal is filled with notes concerning male and female characteristics, coloration, size, range, nest, and Latin names of about forty hummingbird species; these are sometimes accompanied by drawings, made from specimens, with color notes (figs. 11 and 12). He also wrote short texts to accompany the chromolithographs and a fourteen-page draft for an introduction, quoting Audubon's rapturous recital of hummingbird behavior and character and a description of Jamaican hummingbirds by Lady Emmeline Stuart-Wortley, a British poet and author, and including his own observations as well.[8]

However, Heade had difficulty securing the two hundred subscriptions necessary to print his expensive book,[9] and he encountered other problems with the reproduction process itself.[10] Whether it was because he never obtained a sufficient number of subscribers or because he was unhappy with the quality of the chromolithographs, Heade's *Gems of Brazil* was never published. However, in the process, four hummingbird pictures were chromolithographed in trial proofs, each known today in several impressions.

There are some forty-five known paintings of hummingbirds in the *Gems* format — vertical composition, approximately 12 by 10 inches, depicting both the male and female of the species, often near a nest, against landscape backgrounds. These paintings depict about twenty different species. It is clear that in England Heade, to support himself, painted numerous replicas and variations of the original *Gems*, many of which were sold there. As Heade wrote to his friend John R. Bartlett in Providence, Rhode Island, on September 25, 1864: "I doubt whether you'll ever see any of the original Humming Birds, for I can get such prices for them here that I *can't afford* to take them home to sell for one fourth of what I can get here."[11]

The sixteen paintings in the Manoogian Collection (cats. 35–50), framed in groups of four, have been called *The Gems of Brazil* since they were purchased from the family of Kenneth Clark in 1981.[12] These paintings apparently once belonged to Sir Morton Peto, the English railroad magnate and politician, who was known to have owned them by 1879 and who probably purchased them from the artist in London in 1865.[13] However, Heade's book was to be devoted to the hummingbirds of Brazil, and the Peto/Manoogian set puzzlingly includes images of a butterfly (a Brazilian blue morpho), a ruby-throat of North America (which winters in Central America), and a snowcap (fig. 12), which is also found in Central America but not in Brazil. A partial explanation may be found in Heade's draft for the introduction to *The Gems of Brazil*, where he says,

> some cannot be strictly called Brasilian Humming Birds, as their *true habitat* may be the borders of Bolivia, or the Northern States upon the confines of Brasil, but as those that may possibly be the subject of dispute have all been found to range from Potosí [Bolivia] to Caracas, it will not affect the author's purposes to make the small collection exclusively Brasilian, while it admits of his including some of the most brilliant specimens yet discovered.[14]

While Heade mentions birds that may be found in the border states such as the red-tailed comet (cat. 51), he does not admit to including butterflies or Central American birds. Therefore, it seems that although Peto did indeed purchase a set of bird paintings from Heade, these works may not be the "original" group of *Gems* that were exhibited in Rio and later were to be used as the basis for the projected book.

In the *Gems* Heade depicted the male and the female birds perched on tropical plants against lush, often mountainous landscapes. Although Gould's plates often showed tropical flowers, they were apparently chosen purely for their visual appeal.[15] Heade, on the other hand, chose vegetation on the basis of knowledge he had gained by seeing the birds in their native habitat. Among the Manoogian *Gems*, for example, a passion fruit and the opening bud of a passion flower (a flower Heade used in later works, see cats. 55 and 56) are juxtaposed with the ruby-topaz (cat. 35), and a butterfly and pink trumpet flowers (which are fertilized by the hummingbird as it uses its beak to feed on the nectar) are placed with the fork-tailed woodnymph (cat. 42). In the painting of the stripe-breasted starthroat (cat. 45), Heade includes two plants of the bromeliad family, which are plentiful in Brazil and depend on another plant for mechanical support but not nutrients, and in his depiction of the black-eared fairy (cat. 47) he shows the birds with a banana plant at left and a coffee plant at lower right.

As Franklin Kelly has pointed out, "*The Gems* as a series must have been intended to outline the very life cycle of hummingbirds."[16] Thus in the *Hooded Visorbearer* (cat. 43), one sees two birds together who might be courting; in the *Frilled Coquette* (cat. 39), a nest with eggs; in the *Crimson Topaz* (cat. 44), a female sitting on the nest; and in *Amethyst Woodstar* (cat. 38), a nest with two baby hummingbirds.

Heade took particular care in portraying the iridescent quality of hummingbirds' plumage. He applied paint in many layers, and to convey the shimmering quality of the feathers on the throat, cap, or breast, he used a thin glaze over a thick white underlayer of impasto. He achieved a reddish sheen, for instance, by applying a thin glaze of natural rose madder, a red dye derived from the madder root, over a white, reflective, textured underlayer.[17]

Among the four chromolithographs, only one, *Brazilian Hummingbird II*, can be related to its original study, *Two Green-breasted Hummingbirds* (private collection). This painting is thus the only one that can with certainty be identified as one of the original *Gems*. The original painting for the chromolithograph *Brazilian Hummingbirds I* is unlocated.

However, two very close variations exist—*Two Humming-birds with Their Young* (cat. 51) and *Two Hummingbirds Guarding an Egg* (private collection). The pictures differ in the contents of the nest and in the backgrounds. Heade had sketched a male and female red-tailed comet (*Sappho sparga-nura*) in his journal (fig. 11), which he used for these paintings. He wrote in his journal that the sappho was native to Peru and Bolivia but could be found as far south as Mendoza, Argentina, and as far north as Caracas, Venezuela. He also wrote that its nest is loosely attached to a root or twig, as is evident in both paintings. *Two Hummingbirds with Their Young* was bought from Heade by Henry Lippitt, governor of Rhode Island, in about 1865, probably when Lippitt was furnishing his newly completed mansion in Providence.[18]

Two Hummingbirds: Tufted Coquettes, a painting known by Heade's first biographer Robert McIntyre in 1948, but presently unlocated, appears to have been the study for the chromolithograph *Brazilian Hummingbirds III*. Heade depicted the species in two other works in the *Gems* format, *Tufted Coquette* (cat. 40) and *Tufted Coquettes* (private collection). He also sketched the male with its unusual crest and plumes in his journal and included the tufted coquette in *Two Fighting Hummingbirds with Two Orchids* (cat. 60).

One of the birds that Heade especially liked was the horned sun gem (*Heliactin cornuta*) seen in *Two Sun Gems on a Branch* (cat. 52). It is also the bird depicted in the chromolithograph *Brazilian Hummingbird IV*, with the birds posed exactly as in the painting but in a different setting. Heade used this species later in several of his orchid-and-hummingbird pictures and in *Two Hummingbirds Perched on Passion Flower Vines* (cat. 55). In his journal he noted, "This rather rare bird was discovered by the Prince Maximilian in the

Cat. 52 (detail)

interior of Brasil. Very little is known of its habits, & no well authenticated specimen of its nest has yet been found. The female of this bird is the largest, & the tail is longer & has broader feathers than that of the male. Saw but two in Brasil."[19]

Heade painted *Ruby Throat of North America* (cat. 53) in 1865, probably in London. It is similar to the *Ruby-throated Hummingbird* in the Manoogian *Gems* (cat. 49), except that the birds are reversed and surrounded by apple blossoms. Heade painted his first picture of a ruby-throated humming-bird (with nasturtiums, private collection) in 1862 before his trip to Brazil and then three more pictures of this species in 1863, each time coming closer to the *Gems* format. The ruby-throat was one of Heade's favorite species; in his article "Taming Hummingbirds" he wrote, "In the spring all the male birds are in gorgeous attire, and although there are some more magnificent specimens in South America, there are but few more beautiful."[20]

JANET L. COMEY

NOTES

1. Didymus [Martin Johnson Heade], "Taming Hummingbirds," *Forest and Stream* 38, no. 15 (April 14, 1892), p. 348.

2. Martin Johnson Heade, "Brazil/London Journal," manuscript, Museum of Fine Arts, Boston, Gift of Richard and Susanna Nash, 1997.296, p. 13.

3. Ibid., p. 25.

4. Didymus, "Taming Hummingbirds."

5. Heade, "Brazil/London Journal," p. 28.

6. Exposição Geral das Bellas Artes de 1864: Catalogo Explicativo (Rio de Janeiro: Typographia Nacional, 1864), p. 11.

7. The certificate of the decoration was given to the Bucks County Historical Society by Heade's brother in 1915.

8. Martin Johnson Heade, "Introduction to Gems of Brazil," Archives of American Art, Smithsonian Institution, Washington, D.C., reel D5, frames 731-754.

9. Since chromolithography (a color printing process developed in the 1850s, which utilizes a different lithographic stone for each shade) is an expensive process, it was necessary to procure sufficient subscriptions — about 200 — to get the book printed. Roger F. Pasquier and John Farrand, Jr., *Masterpieces of Bird Art: Seven Hundred Years of Ornithological Illustration* (New York: Abbeville Press, 1991), p. 116. Although Heade had secured some fifty subscribers in Brazil, he had a more difficult time in England.

10. Trial proofs by Day & Son, another leading lithographic printing firm, were not satisfactory, causing Heade to express his doubts about the project: "But to tell you the truth I am not at all satisfied that it is yet on the right track. The two more completed [proofs] are very well when re-touched by hand, but I want to get rid of the necessity of that. I told Day this morning that it was useless to think of having the book printed & bound here if all the plates must be retouched." May 24, 1864, Heade to John R. Bartlett, John Russell Bartlett Papers, John Carter Brown Library, Brown University, Providence, Rhode Island.

11. Heade to Bartlett, from London, September 25, 1864.

12. This group was purchased by Reid & Lefevre Gallery, London; Hirschl & Adler Galleries, Inc., New York; and Coe Kerr Gallery, New York. The Peto/Manoogian *Gems* were apparently purchased at a country auction in England before World War II by Lord Kenneth Clark, the eminent art connoisseur and former director of the National Gallery of London, and descended in his family until 1981.

13. It was reported by Clement and Hutton in 1879 that Heade "went to Brazil with the intention of publishing an illustrated book on the Humming-Birds of South America, a work which he was forced to abandon after a year's effort on account of the difficulties experienced in the proper execution of the chromos. The original designs, frequently exhibited, were purchased by Sir Morton Peto, and are now in London." Clara Erskine Clement and Laurence Hutton, *Artists of the Nineteenth Century and Their Works* (Boston: Houghton, Osgood and Company, 1879), vol. 1, p. 340. It was also reported in John Denison Champlin, Jr., ed., *Cyclopedia of Painters and Paintings* (New York: Charles Scribner's Sons, 1886), p. 219, that "His Brazilian sketches, originally intended for a book on South American Humming-Birds, are now owned by Sir Morton Peto, London."

14. Heade, "Introduction to Gems of Brazil."

15. Pasquier and Farrand, *Masterpieces of Bird Art*, p. 142.

16. See Franklin Kelly's excellent entry on *The Gems of Brazil* in *American Paintings from the Manoogian Collection*, exh. cat. (Washington, D.C.: National Gallery of Art, 1989), p. 118.

17. I am grateful to Elizabeth Leto Fulton for sharing her study of Heade's techniques with me.

18. Charles Richard Steedman, grandson of Governor Lippitt, to Theodore E. Stebbins, Jr., April 15, 1968.

19. Heade, "Brazil/London Journal," unpaginated section.

20. Didymus, "Taming Hummingbirds."

35

RUBY-TOPAZ, *about 1864–65*

Manoogian Collection

36

BRAZILIAN RUBY, *about 1864–65*

Manoogian Collection

79

37

BLACK-THROATED MANGO, *about 1864–65*

Manoogian Collection

38

AMETHYST WOODSTAR, *about 1864–65*

Manoogian Collection

39

FRILLED COQUETTE, *about 1864–65*

Manoogian Collection

40

TUFTED COQUETTE, *about 1864–65*

Manoogian Collection

41

BLACK-BREASTED PLOVERCREST, *about 1864–65*

Manoogian Collection

42

FORK-TAILED WOODNYMPH, *about 1864–65*

Manoogian Collection

43

HOODED VISORBEARER, *about 1864–65*

Manoogian Collection

44

CRIMSON TOPAZ, *about 1864–65*

Manoogian Collection

45

STRIPE-BREASTED STARTHROAT, *about 1864–65*

Manoogian Collection

46

SNOWCAP, *about 1864–65*

Manoogian Collection

47

Manoogian Collection

48

WHITE-VENTED VIOLET-EAR, *about 1864–65*

Manoogian Collection

49

RUBY-THROATED HUMMINGBIRD, *about 1864–65*

Manoogian Collection

50

BLUE MORPHO BUTTERFLY, *about 1864–65*

Manoogian Collection

51

TWO HUMMINGBIRDS WITH THEIR YOUNG, *about 1864–65*

Jerald Dillon Fessenden

52

TWO SUN GEMS ON A BRANCH, *about 1864–65*

Manoogian Collection

53

RUBY THROAT OF NORTH AMERICA, *1865*

Private Collection

AFTER HIS THIRD AND FINAL TRIP to Latin America in 1870, when he visited Colombia, Panama, and Jamaica, Heade began to make larger, more complex compositions combining hummingbirds and tropical flowers in landscapes. These works were an outgrowth of his *Gems of Brazil* project, where he painted the hummingbird pairs in their natural habitats in small formats. As suggested by Ella Foshay, Heade's increasingly integrated view of nature may have been influenced by the contemporary writings of Charles Darwin.[1]

Heade painted only ten known compositions that include hummingbirds and passion flowers.[2] The first, the sole dated picture, was executed in 1870; in 1895 he apparently was still working with the subject. An article in the St. Augustine *Tatler* noted the presence in Heade's studio of "[a] new and brilliant picture [of] the scarlet passion flower, as it grows in the jungles, brilliant beyond compare."[3] For the most part, however, the passion flower paintings elicited little contemporary comment from the press, and they seldom appeared in nineteenth-century exhibitions.[4]

Tropical Landscape with Ten Hummingbirds, 1870 (cat. 54), is unique in Heade's oeuvre. In a complex composition of intertwined vines, leaves, and tendrils snaking from tree branch to tree branch across the foreground, Heade depicted ten colorful birds from eight species (there are two male-and-female pairs).[5] The brilliant greens and yellows of the birds, most of which are perched facing alternating directions, contrast with the bright red passion flower buds. The spread wings and tail of the fork-tailed woodnymph at the upper right, the only bird in flight, echoes the shape of the solitary open passion flower blossom below. The whole of this extraordinary display is set against a view of a tropical lake and distant mountains, similar in composition to the later *Coast of Jamaica* (fig. 13).

Native to Brazil, Peru, Colombia, Jamaica, and the West Indies, these eight species would never have appeared together in one place. Although the arrangement of the birds is artificial, their habitat is realistic. As Charles Darwin had observed, hummingbird beaks were specially suited to fertilizing passion flowers.[6] In addition, passion flowers grew wild in tropical climates, and probably Heade had first observed the *Passiflora racemosa*, which he depicted here, in Brazil.[7]

Although Heade included the passion flower as a part of the hummingbirds' natural environment, the Christian iconography of the plant would have been apparent to him and his contemporaries.[8] Associated with the Passion of Christ since its introduction to Europe in the seventeenth century, the passion flower acquired its name because of the resemblance of its corona filaments to the crown of thorns. The three stigma, then, represented the nails, and the ten sepals and petals, the ten apostles present at the crucifixion (excluding

Fig. 13. *Coast of Jamaica*, 1874, oil on canvas. Museum of Fine Arts, Boston, Gift of Mrs. Katherine H. Putnam and the John Pickering Lyman Collection, by exchange, in memory of Maxim Karolik, 1981.363.

Peter and Judas).[9] In the nineteenth century passion flowers were cultivated in Europe in both private greenhouses and botanical gardens.[10] Their popularity was such that they were even included in ladies' bouquets and floral centerpieces.[11]

Tropical Landscape with Ten Hummingbirds relates to the established tradition of seventeenth-century Dutch still life, which in its broadest definition included live animals as subject matter.[12] Artists such as Melchior de Hondecoeter and Jan van Kessel the Elder painted groups of live birds in domestic or exotic landscapes. Heade also may have known of Dutch-influenced English artists such as the animal and botanical painter Philip Reinagle (1749–1833). Reinagle's large *Humming Birds* (fig. 14), which sets over thirty birds in an allegedly South American landscape, is intriguingly similar to Heade's extraordinary composition.[13]

Heade never repeated the fantastic *Tropical Landscape with Ten Hummingbirds*. His reasons for attempting it remain unknown; possibly it was a commission. He went on, however,

Fig. 14. Philip Reinagle (1749-1833), *Humming Birds*, about 1786, oil on canvas. Private Collection.

Fig. 15. *The Jamaica Sketchbook: Study of Passion Flowers*, about 1870, graphite on paper. Museum of Fine Arts, Boston, Gift of Richard and Susanna Nash, 1997.297.

Fig. 16. *Study of Passion Flower Leaves*, about 1870, oil on canvas (unstretched). St. Augustine Historical Society, St. Augustine, Florida.

to experiment with different combinations of passion flowers and hummingbirds in paintings that featured simpler compositions with fewer birds, usually only one or two.[14]

For the flower, he continued to favor the red *Passiflora racemosa*, the species he had used in *Tropical Landscape with Ten Hummingbirds* and which he had sketched both in pencil and in oil during his 1870 trip to the tropics (figs. 15 and 16).[15] In *Two Hummingbirds Perched on Passion Flower Vines* (cat. 55), as in *Tropical Landscape with Ten Hummingbirds*, Heade contrasted the passion flowers to the colorful birds, but here with only two males — a sun gem and a red-tailed comet. Less entangled vines with fewer leaves and buds drape down the right side of the picture following the vertical orientation of the canvas and then wind across the lower portion of the fore-

ground. The center of the composition is left open; this sparer arrangement focuses on the dramatic colors of the two birds and the two open flowers.

Finally, in *Passion Flowers and Hummingbirds* (cat. 56) Heade adopted a more muted palette, creating perhaps the most evocative of all his hummingbird-and-passion-flower pictures. Vines snake boldly across the foreground in a twisted X-shape, but Heade painted the passion flowers in a less intense red and included a pair of black-and-white snowcaps. The tiny black-and-white birds, set against the atmospheric background, are less noticeable than the blossoms, whose sensuous, dramatic beauty is emphasized.

KAREN E. QUINN

NOTES

1. Ella Foshay, *Reflections of Nature: Flowers in American Art*, exh. cat. (New York: Whitney Museum of American Art, 1984), pp. 52-57.

2. Two, which include the small *Passiflora alata*, also feature orchids; see n. 15.

3. "Chit-Chat. An Hour with the Artists," St. Augustine *Tatler*, March 2, 1895, p. 2.

4. In 1876 Heade exhibited a work entitled *Scarlet Passion Flower* at the Brooklyn Art Association; *Night-Blooming Cereus and Scarlet Passion Flowers* (unlocated since the nineteenth century) was exhibited prior to auction at Schenck's Art Gallery in New York, according to the *New York Evening Post*, March 21, 1876, p. 3; and in 1877 *Passion Flower* was exhibited at the National Academy of Design and *Scarlet Passion Flower* at the Brooklyn Art Association.

5. The birds, all males except as noted, can be identified as follows, beginning at the upper center of the picture and proceeding clockwise: red-tailed comet (*Sappho sparganura*); horned sun gem (*Heliactin cornuta*); forked-tail woodnymph (*Thalurania furcata*; in flight); male and female tufted coquette (*Lophornis ornata*); male and female crimson topaz (*Topaza pella*); black-eared fairy (*Heliothryx aurita*) at the lower center of the composition; a ruby topaz (*Chrysolampis mosquitus*); and a western streamertail (*Trochilus polytmus*) at the far left. All but one of the birds had appeared in the earlier, small-format *Gems of Brazil* paintings; the western streamertail, native to Jamaica and probably new to Heade from his recent trip, did not.

6. Charles Darwin, *The Effects of Cross and Self Fertilisation in the Vegetable Kingdom* (London, 1876), pp. 370-371, as cited in Foshay, *Reflections of Nature,* pp. 56 and 185 n. 82.

7. Over 200 passion flower species were known in the nineteenth century; over 450 are known today. See John Vanderplanck, *Passion Flowers*, 2d ed. (Cambridge, Mass.: MIT Press, 1996), p. 9.

8. Theodore E. Stebbins, Jr., *The Life and Works of Martin Johnson Heade* (New Haven, Conn.: Yale University Press, 1975), p. 149.

9. Vanderplanck, *Passion Flowers*, pp. 202-205.

10. Ibid., p. 7.

11. Jennifer Davies, *The Victorian Flower Garden* (London: BBC Books, 1991), pp. 168-169, 204, 207.

12. On still life, see Edith Greindl, *Les Peintres flamandes de nature morte au XVIIe siècle* (Sterrebeck, Belgium: Editions d'Art Michel Lefebvre, 1983).

13. According to the owner, the landscape has traditionally been identified as that of South America. Philip Reinagle also did paintings from which prints were made for Dr. John Robert Thornton's *Temple of Flora* (1799-1807), including the "Large Flowering Sensitive Plant," which included hummingbirds and a mountainous landscape.

14. In one case Heade depicted three birds, *Passion Flowers with Three Hummingbirds* (San Antonio Museum of Art).

15. The *Passiflora alata*, which Heade had also sketched in pencil, appears in two compositions that also include orchids: *White Orchid and Hummingbird* (private collection) and *Orchids, Passion Flowers and Hummingbird* (private collection).

54

TROPICAL LANDSCAPE WITH TEN HUMMINGBIRDS, *1870*

Roy Nutt Family Trust

55

TWO HUMMINGBIRDS PERCHED ON

PASSION FLOWER VINES,

about 1870–83

Private Collection

56

PASSION FLOWERS AND HUMMINGBIRDS, *about 1870–83*

Museum of Fine Arts, Boston

ORCHIDS

IN JANUARY 1871 both the *New York Evening Post* and the *Boston Daily Evening Transcript* reported, "M. J. Heade's last finished work presents a study of the flower of the South American 'Orchid' or air plant, with hummingbirds poising over it, drawn against a tropical background."[1] This matter-of-fact announcement does not in any way indicate the significance of Heade's new subject — an original combination of flowers and birds in a natural landscape, about which historians have agreed that "there are quite simply no other paintings like these known in America or elsewhere."[2]

Today, some fifty-five orchid-and-hummingbird paintings by Heade, the earliest dated 1871, the last, 1902, survive, and it is likely that others have been lost. Undoubtedly Heade had first seen orchids growing wild in Brazil in 1863 and surely also knew of the descriptions of them in the writings of Alexander von Humboldt, Louis Agassiz, and James Cooley Fletcher. In his unpublished introduction to *The Gems of Brazil* of about 1864-65, Heade discussed whether certain hummingbird beaks were specially shaped to extract insects or honey from "cup-shaped" orchids.[3] Many of *The Gems of Brazil*, the series of small hummingbird pictures of the mid-1860s, include flowers, but the large cattleya orchid becomes an element in his work only after his third and final Latin American trip to Panama, Colombia, and Jamaica in 1870. It was probably on that journey that he sketched orchids in pencil and in oil (fig. 17 and cat. 64),

and it was also at that time he conceived a new series of works combining orchids and hummingbirds in dramatic fashion.[4]

Orchids enjoyed great popularity in Europe and the United States in the nineteenth century. William Cattley's successful experiments in 1818 with the plant that was ultimately named for him, the *Cattleya labiata* (which became Heade's favorite), mark the beginning of orchid cultivation on a grand scale in England.[5] In the United States, orchids were first cultivated in Boston in the 1830s.[6] Developments in the regulation of temperatures in greenhouses further advanced both British and American orchid growing during these years. Books such as John Lindley's *Genera and Species of Orchidaceous Plants* (London, 1830-40), James Bateman's *Orchidaceae of Mexico and Guatemala* (London, 1837-43; and later his *Second Century of Orchidaceous Plants* [London, 1867]), Charles Darwin's *Various Contrivances by Which British and Foreign Orchids are Fertilised by Insects* (London, 1862), and Edward Rand's *Orchids. A Description of the Species and Varieties Grown at Glen Ridge, near Boston* (New York, 1876) all contributed to furthering both scientific knowledge and the general popularity of orchids. By midcentury, amateur botanists grew them, and they were even worn as lapel flowers and used in bouquets.[7]

Orchids were also associated with sexuality, which may account for the scant notice Heade's paintings of them elicited during his lifetime.[8] Named after the Greek *orchis*, for testi-

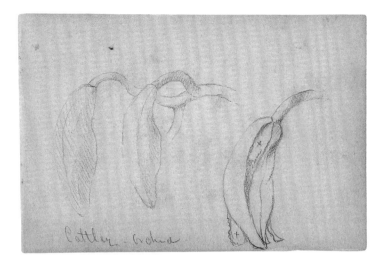

Fig. 17. *The Jamaica Sketchbook: "Cattley[a] Orchid,"* about 1870, graphite on paper. Museum of Fine Arts, Boston, Gift of Richard and Susanna Nash, 1997.297.

cle, probably after the shape of a tuber at the base of the flower of certain species, orchids were considered an aphrodisiac in antiquity. Despite this heritage, or perhaps because of it, the many nineteenth-century flower books, often with titles such as *Flora's Lexicon*, rarely mention the orchid or its symbolic meaning.

The originality of Heade's orchid-and-hummingbird compositions lies not in combining birds and flowers, or even the inclusion of landscape backgrounds, for these devices were already established in ornithological illustration in the nineteenth century, as Heade would have known from his studies of the hummingbird literature. Heade's inventiveness came in combining dramatic, enlarged foreground flowers with (usually) a pair of hummingbirds before an evocative, believable tropical landscape. The result was a new kind of painting, equally still life and landscape, which possessed great sensual and emotional power.

Heade established the format for his orchid-and-hummingbird compositions in his earliest paintings of the subject. In *Cattleya Orchid and Three Brazilian Hummingbirds* (cat.

57) and *Orchid with Two Hummingbirds* (cat. 58), both dated 1871, the birds and flowers are placed in the foreground, close to the picture plane, looming large but painted to actual scale. The orchid plant grows naturally out of a dense, tropical forest. In each of these paintings, the same asymmetrically positioned pink *Cattleya labiata* flower is featured. In *Cattleya Orchid and Three Brazilian Hummingbirds*, Heade depicted a male and female amethyst woodstar protecting their nest from a red-tailed comet.[9] In *Orchid with Two Hummingbirds* Heade simplified the composition and used two colorful male birds, a red-tailed comet and a black-eared fairy. All of his subsequent orchid-and-hummingbird paintings featured only one or two birds, and, as he experimented with the subject, Heade gradually moved away from the brilliantly plumed species in favor of birds with less intense colors that harmonized better with the hues of the flowers.

In these first efforts birds and orchid plant exist independently of each other, as if separate vignettes. In the fully developed works, such as *Two Fighting Hummingbirds with Two Orchids*, 1875 (cat. 60), Heade integrates flora, fauna, and the mountainous setting. The sinuous forms of two cattleya orchids, one seen from the front and the other from the back, are echoed by the pair of buds and, at left, by two battling male birds of different species. A sudden thunderstorm sweeps over the jungle, while mountains are seen in the distance. It is as if the painter had climbed into the trees to witness a scene both intimate and grand, one that is highly charged with natural energy.

Heade continued to experiment with the compositions of his orchid-and-hummingbird paintings, trying out different combinations of birds and flowers and a variety of settings. In *Fighting Hummingbirds with Pink Orchid* (cat. 59, in the less typical vertical format), Heade pulled the birds and orchid close together and cut off the distance with dense foliage,

Opposite: Cat. 60 (detail)

creating a private glimpse into the natural world. In *Orchid and Hummingbirds near a Mountain Lake* (cat. 61), the pair of black-eared fairies and the orchid blossom are tightly composed in the center, set against a distant view of the mountains and lake. Heade used the same flower in these two paintings, as if traced or somehow transferred; this identical orchid appears in twenty-one known works.

Heade's exploration of color in his orchid-and-hummingbird pictures is also evident in the canvases in which he used orchids other than the pink *Cattleya labiata*. In five vertically oriented paintings including *An Amethyst Hummingbird with a White Orchid* (cat. 63), he painted the white-and-purple *Lealia purpurata*, the national flower of Brazil. The blossoms in each of the five compositions are based on the oil sketch *Study of Lealia Purpurata and Another Orchid* (cat. 64). In *An Amethyst Hummingbird with a White Orchid* Heade juxtaposed the flower to an amethyst woodstar, whose colors echo, rather than contrast with, those of the orchid.

Finally, Heade used the pale-gold-and-purple *Cattleya dowiana*, native to Costa Rica and northern Colombia, in three compositions. In *Orchids and Hummingbird* (cat. 62), Heade painted a single amethyst woodstar and two *Cattleya dowiana* blooms. The magenta interior of the orchid blossoms is echoed in the throat of the hummingbird in a magnificent three-way orchestration of tones, unifying the relationship between flowers and bird. Heade's sensitivity to color was described in a rare contemporaneous critique of one of his orchid paintings, "A delicate, large pink orchid, with its leaves growing by a mossy piece of wood, led the eye by the forms of pink humming-birds, as delicate as itself, into the gray distance of a landscape. Here on the hazy hill-side this pink was again repeated like an echo of the foreground color, by stray sunbeams falling through the mist."[10]

KAREN E. QUINN

NOTES

1. "Art Notes," *New York Evening Post*, January 27, 1871, p. 2; and "New York Art Items," *Boston Daily Evening Transcript*, January 28, 1871, p. 3.

2. Theodore E. Stebbins, Jr., *The Life and Works of Martin Johnson Heade* (New Haven, Conn.: Yale University Press, 1975), p. 148. See also Ella Milbank Foshay, *Nineteenth-Century American Flower Painting and the Botanical Sciences*, Ph.D. diss., Columbia University, 1979 (Ann Arbor, Mich.: UMI Research Press, 1981), p. 304.

3. Introduction, Martin Johnson Heade Papers, Archives of American Art, Smithsonian Institution, Washington, D.C., reel D5, frames 731-754.

4. Stebbins, *Martin Johnson Heade*, pp. 146-147, suggests the oil sketches may have been done in New York.

5. Alec Pridgeon, ed., *The Illustrated Encyclopedia of Orchids* (Portland, Oreg.: Timber Press, 1992), p. 14.

6. Stebbins, *Martin Johnson Heade*, p. 138, and Foshay, *Nineteenth-Century American Flower Painting*, p. 302.

7. Jennifer Davies, *The Victorian Flower Garden* (London: BBC Books, 1991), pp. 163, 169, 177.

8. Stebbins, *Martin Johnson Heade*, pp. 138-139.

9. The inclusion of three birds is a rarity but one Heade had experimented with briefly in small format in 1866. *Hummingbirds: Two Sun Gems and a Crimson Topaz* (Shelburne Museum, Shelburne, Vt.) also shows a male and female guarding their nest from a third, larger bird.

10. "The Arts. At the Studios," *Appleton's Journal of Literature, Science, and Art* 13 (March 27, 1875), p. 410.

57

CATTLEYA ORCHID AND THREE BRAZILIAN HUMMINGBIRDS, *1871*

National Gallery of Art, Washington

58

ORCHID WITH TWO HUMMINGBIRDS, *1871*

Reynolda House, Museum of American Art, Winston-Salem, North Carolina

59

FIGHTING HUMMINGBIRDS WITH PINK ORCHID, *about 1875–90*

Private Collection, Kingston, Massachusetts

60

TWO FIGHTING HUMMINGBIRDS WITH TWO ORCHIDS, *1875*

Private Collection

61

ORCHID AND HUMMINGBIRDS NEAR A MOUNTAIN LAKE, *about 1875–90*

Private Collection

62

ORCHIDS AND HUMMINGBIRD, *about 1875–83*

Museum of Fine Arts, Boston

63

AN AMETHYST HUMMINGBIRD

WITH A WHITE ORCHID,

about 1875–90

Jo Ann and Julian Ganz, Jr.

64

STUDY OF LEALIA PURPURATA AND ANOTHER ORCHID, *about 1870*

St. Augustine Historical Society

FLORIDA: THE LATE WORK

$\mathcal{I}$N MARCH 1883, after years of constant traveling, Heade settled in St. Augustine, Florida, and in September of the same year, at the age of sixty-four, married Elizabeth Smith, a woman from Long Island some twenty years his junior. Henry Morrison Flagler, John D. Rockefeller's partner in the Standard Oil Company, also discovered St. Augustine at about this time and not only changed the city but also greatly affected Heade's life. Determined to make St. Augustine the "Newport of the South," Flagler built the magnificent Hotel Ponce de Leon, which opened in January 1888. Flagler also added a suite of seven artists' studios at the rear of the hotel, where the artists held weekly receptions. For the rest of his life, Heade occupied Studio 7 and reportedly welcomed visitors at all times.[1] In addition to supplying Heade with a steady stream of potential buyers, Flagler in 1887 commissioned him to paint two large landscapes for his hotel—*View from Fern-Tree Walk, Jamaica* (cat. 24) and *The Great Florida Sunset* (fig. 44)—paying him two thousand dollars for each. In addition, he bought at least a dozen other works from Heade.

Of the approximately 150 known pictures Heade painted from 1883 until his death in 1904, some two-thirds are still lifes, one-third are landscapes, and two are portraits.[2] Although he continued to paint northern marsh scenes, Heade was particularly inspired by the nearby marshes and the St. Johns River, the largest and most important river in Florida. One of the few North American rivers to flow north, the St. Johns arises in the middle of the peninsula, parallels the east coast, and enters the Atlantic Ocean north of Jacksonville. Because it is navigable for some two hundred miles, tourists have been plying the river on steamers since the middle of the nineteenth century. It is probably the St. Johns River that Heade depicted in *Florida River Scene* (cat. 73). Heade deftly painted the patches of light on the palm trees to the left and the reflection in the gently flowing river of the passing storm and the red-tinged clouds. As he had in his northern marsh scenes, he imparted a sense of spaciousness and depth through the recession of the river to the sailboat in the distance in this horizontal composition. Although the painting's early history is unknown, from 1958 until the early 1970s the picture hung in one of the salons on the SS *Brasil* (Moore-McCormack Lines, Inc.) as it made regular crossings between New York and South America's east coast.[3]

Heade was captivated by the orange blossoms, Cherokee roses, and magnolias growing in Florida, just as earlier he had been fascinated by the orchids and passion flowers he saw in Latin America. He made several oil sketches of the Cherokee rose (*Rosa laevigata*), including *Branches of Cherokee Roses* (cat. 65) as well as numerous finished compositions of this flower. The St. Augustine *Tatler* praised Heade's "studies of the Cherokee rose that grows so profusely here, climbing over stumps and hedges, transforming them into things of beauty," describing them as "wonderfully like; the pure white petals, yellow stamens and glossy, dark leaves are so natural as to deceive."[4] Although the rampantly growing Cherokee rose appears to be indigenous to the southern states, it originated in China. It has never been explained how it got to the United States, but was discovered in Georgia by the French explorer André Michaux in 1803.[5] Many Cherokee Indian legends and traditions involve these roses, which were the only flowers that braves gathered for their brides to make garlands for their hair. Wearing these flowers ensured the brides' happiness with their husbands.[6]

Branches of Cherokee Roses is one of twenty-four oil sketches owned by the St. Augustine Historical Society.[7] Heade gave this group of studies to a young art student, Wilma E. Davis, in the early 1900s, and she in turn presented them to the Historical Society in 1944. Heade executed these works from life, probably shortly after arriving in Florida; he later used them in making numerous finished paintings, many of which make literal, exact use of the sketches. *Branches of Cherokee Roses* has the appearance of having been painted out-of-doors, in bright sunlight that casts shadows on the blossoms and creates highlights on the glossy leaves.

For the majority of his Cherokee rose still lifes, Heade chose horizontal compositions, placing the flowers on table-tops on plush velvet. However, he also employed some vertical compositions, where the roses are in glass tumblers or in vases on plush-covered tables, as with *White Cherokee Roses in a Salamander Vase* (cat. 67). This composition is twice as tall as wide, and here the painter has put the vase slightly off-center, in the corner of a room. In this tour de force the roses themselves are shown in various stages of maturity, from closed buds to completely open blossoms, and from many different angles. Light defines the corner in the background, the sinuous curve of the salamander on the vase, the shiny leaves, and the rich velvet. In addition to the complex arrangement of the roses, he painted a variety of textures, including the metal on the vase, the water within the vase, the waxy leaves, soft petals, and luxurious velvet. Probably executed sometime about 1890, *White Cherokee Roses in a Salamander Vase* proves that even at this late date Heade had lost neither skill nor innovative powers.

A survey of his remarkable magnolia paintings further demonstrates Heade's undiminished vigor. Heade painted some five oil sketches and seventeen finished paintings of the *Magnolia grandiflora*, the best-known American magnolia, which is native to the southeastern coastal region. Bearing large white flowers, this hardy evergreen is truly a handsome tree, but only one major American artist, John La Farge, had painted the magnolia before Heade began his series.[8] La Farge executed three paintings of single magnolia blossoms in vases in the early 1860s.[9] However, La Farge's magnolias are more painterly than Heade's, as Kathleen Foster has written: "Unlike Heade's voluptuous, highly-detailed magnolias and orchids, La Farge's flowers tend toward generalization; botanical detail, surface texture and the 'image-content' of the flower itself are almost obliterated in favor of artistic problems based on color, light and structure alone."[10]

Although Heade painted three pictures of magnolias in vases, the majority of his magnolia paintings are horizontal with the cut branches and flowers arranged on red, brown, or blue velvet, an innovative compositional format. Exploiting the contrast between the milky white petals and the red velvet, Heade depicted one blossom in *A Magnolia on Red Velvet* (cat. 68) and two blossoms in *Magnoliae Grandiflorae* (cat. 72) of 1888, the only painting of this series in this exhibition to bear a date. Although it is impossible to know in what order Heade painted the works, the magnolias on blue velvet with three blossoms seem to be the culmination of the series. In *Giant Magnolias* from the R. W. Norton Art Gallery (cat. 70) and

Giant Magnolias on a Blue Velvet Cloth from the National Gallery of Art (cat. 71) three flowers in various stages of development suggest the passing of time as if we are watching a single blossom slowly unfold. Further, as Franklin Kelly has remarked concerning these two paintings, "[T]hey do seem to depict two moments in time. That all the flowers are open in the [Norton] picture suggests they are slightly older than in the Gallery's version. This impression is supported by the appearance of the leaves."[11]

In painting these works Heade frequently relied on his oil sketches for individual blossoms. For example, Heade transferred (or traced) the large blossom on the right in *Study of Three Blossoms of Magnolia* (cat. 66) to the Norton and National Gallery pictures. From the same oil sketch he used the top flower in the National Gallery painting and the bottom left magnolia in the Norton picture. However, although the same sketch is the basis for these two paintings, they differ not only in terms of the ripeness of the branch but also in the impression conveyed by the subtle differences in color and the depths of the shadows.

In 1898 St. Augustine's *Tatler* reported, "Mr. Heade frequently uses a rich plush as a back ground, painting it most exquisitely and effectively and adding greatly to the beauty of the blossoms."[12] William Gerdts has noted that Heade used a velvet ground more extensively than any other artist.[13] The sensuousness of this soft fabric contrasting with the fleshy white petals and lustrous green leaves of the recumbent flower has prompted scholars to remark on the latent sexuality of the magnolia images. Whether Heade intended sexual overtones is not clear. However, as Kelly has written, "the mysteriously shadowed interior space, the lush colors, full, curving contours, overall sense of opulence, and implied perfumed scent of the flowers make them deeply suggestive."[14]

Although the magnolia paintings received little attention from the critics during his lifetime, the sensuality and mysteriousness of the series have been remarked on since Heade's rediscovery in the 1940s. Robert McIntyre, Heade's first biographer, wondered if they had overtones of death or unrequited affection. In 1948 he wrote, "What strange indwelling force drove him to cast out a simple flower in the white perfection of its bloom, to wither and die. . . . There is a strange fusion here of objective realism and the release of pent-up emotions. But whatever the impulse, whatever the intention, this is one of the most stirring incidents in the whole realm of American art."[15] John I. H. Baur captured the sensuousness of the paintings in 1954 with his often-quoted description: "the fleshly whiteness of magnolia blossoms startlingly arrayed on sumptuous red velvet like odalisques on a couch."[16] In 1980 Barbara Novak compared Heade's magnolias with Church's plant studies in formal terms: "Heade's glossy flowers achieve the quality of becoming through their writhing linear gestures; Church's, from the immediacy of the paint. . . . Yet Heade's smooth surfaces also embalm his subjects in a crystalline time."[17]

The growing recognition of the importance of the magnolia paintings was reinforced when *Giant Magnolias on a Blue Velvet Cloth* (cat. 71) was included in the 1983 exhibition *A New World: Masterpieces of American Painting, 1760–1910*. The series is now considered as significant as the thunderstorm subjects, the marshes, and the orchid-and-hummingbird pictures. These works, executed in an anachronistic, highly realistic style near the end of the nineteenth century, are increasingly admired not only for their lush beauty and sensuousness but also for their mysterious, darker qualities.

JANET L. COMEY

NOTES

1. "A Reception at the Ponce de Leon Studios," St. Augustine *Tatler*, March 31, 1894, p. 10. Among the artists occupying the other studios in 1889 were the New England artists George Seavey, a flower painter; Frank Henry Shapleigh and W. Staples Drown, both painters of St. Augustine views; the German artist Robert S. German, landscapist and portraitist; and later, the Philadelphia artist Felix deCrano, landscape and still-life painter. See Frederic A. Sharf, "St. Augustine: City of Artists, 1883–1895," *The Magazine Antiques* 90, no. 2 (August 1966), pp. 220–223.

2. In about 1898 Heade painted portraits of Dr. Andrew Anderson, a leading citizen of St. Augustine (private collection, on loan to Flagler College, St. Augustine), and of William Howland Pell, a regular winter visitor from New York (unlocated).

3. "General Description of Murals, Paintings and Sculpture on the S. S. Brasil," Moore-McCormack Lines, Inc., 1958, p. 4. We are grateful to David Hendrickson for bringing this information to our attention.

4. "Ponce de Leon Studios," St. Augustine *Tatler*, February 5, 1898, p. 5.

5. Bruce Weber, *American Beauty: The Rose in American Art, 1800–1920*, exh. cat. (New York: Berry-Hill Galleries, 1997), p. 21.

6. Jean Gordon, *Pageant of the Rose* (New York: Studio Publications, 1953), p. 12.

7. See *Martin Johnson Heade: The Floral and Hummingbird Studies from the St. Augustine Historical Society*, exh. cat. (Boca Raton: Boca Raton Museum of Art, 1992).

8. An intriguing exception are two watercolors of the *Magnolia grandiflora* (about 1872-74, Stowe-Day Foundation, Hartford, Conn.) by Harriet Beecher Stowe, renowned as the author of *Uncle Tom's Cabin* but also an artist. See Joseph S. Van Why, "History in Houses: The Harriet Beecher Stowe House in Nook Farm," *The Magazine Antiques* 94, no. 3 (September 1968), cover illus., pp. 343, 379. Stowe's brother, the Reverend Henry Ward Beecher, owned at least one Heade painting, and Stowe herself recommended "that lovely golden twilight sketch of Heade's" for decorating a room in her *House and Home Papers* (Boston: Fields, Osgood, & Co., 1869), p. 95.

9. See James L. Yarnall, *Nature Vivante: The Still Lifes of John La Farge*, exh. cat. (New York: The Jordan-Volpe Gallery, 1995), pp. 120–121.

10. Kathleen A. Foster, "The Still-Life Paintings of John La Farge," *American Art Journal* 11, no. 3 (summer 1979), p. 25.

11. Franklin Kelly et al., *American Paintings of the Nineteenth Century, Part I* (Washington, D.C.: National Gallery of Art, 1996), p. 296.

12. "Ponce de Leon Studios," St. Augustine *Tatler*, February 5, 1898, p. 5.

13. William H. Gerdts and Russell Burke, *American Still-Life Painting* (New York: Praeger, 1971), p. 97.

14. Kelly et al., *American Paintings of the Nineteenth Century*, p. 296.

15. Robert D. McIntyre, *Martin Johnson Heade* (New York: Pantheon Press, 1948), p. 47.

16. John I. H. Baur, Introduction, *Commemorative Exhibition: Paintings by M. J. Heade and F. H. Lane from the Private Collection of Maxim Karolik and the M. and M. Karolik Collection of American Paintings from the Museum of Fine Arts, Boston*, exh. cat. (New York: M. Knoedler and Company, 1954), unpaginated.

17. Barbara Novak, *Nature and Culture: American Landscape and Painting, 1825–1875* (New York: Oxford University Press, 1980), p. 122.

65

BRANCHES OF CHEROKEE ROSES, *about 1883–88*

St. Augustine Historical Society

STUDY OF THREE BLOSSOMS OF MAGNOLIA, *about 1883–88*

St. Augustine Historical Society

67

WHITE CHEROKEE ROSES IN A SALAMANDER VASE,

about 1883–1895

James W. and Frances G. McGlothlin

68

A MAGNOLIA ON RED VELVET, *about 1885–1895*

Teresa Heinz and the Late Senator John Heinz

69

TWO MAGNOLIAS AND A BUD ON TEAL VELVET, *about 1885–1895*

James W. and Frances G. McGlothlin

70

GIANT MAGNOLIAS, *about 1885–1895*

The R. W. Norton Art Gallery, Shreveport, Louisiana

71

GIANT MAGNOLIAS ON A BLUE VELVET CLOTH, *about 1885–1895*

National Gallery of Art, Washington

72

MAGNOLIAE GRANDIFLORAE, *1888*

Jo Ann and Julian Ganz, Jr.

73

FLORIDA RIVER SCENE, *about 1887–1900 (detail overleaf)*

Private Collection

PICTURING HEADE: THE PAINTER AND HIS CRITICS

---

*M*ARTIN JOHNSON HEADE's contemporaries would be astonished to find that his paintings are highly regarded and much studied in the late twentieth century. In his own day, this much-traveled artist earned only a modest reputation along with just enough patronage to enable him to paint for over sixty-five years. A few lines were devoted to his work in the two major books of the 1860s that surveyed American art, by Henry T. Tuckerman and James Jackson Jarves,[1] and his pictures attracted frequent though commonly brief notices in the press throughout his career; in general, the critics were complimentary toward his work but on occasion could be harshly critical of it. Heade counted among his friends and patrons a number of prominent people, but there is no evidence that anyone during Heade's lifetime considered him a painter of major stature.

In 1839 Heade painted his earliest known work, *Portrait of a Young Lady* (see fig. 1), when he was twenty years old. His work was first shown publicly when another portrait (unlocated) was exhibited two years later at the Pennsylvania Academy of the Fine Arts in Philadelphia. A decade afterward, in 1851, after stays in New York, Trenton, Richmond, Philadelphia, and Rome, he was working in St. Louis, where he received the first public recognition of which we are aware, when the *Western Journal and Civilian* proclaimed itself "moved with admiration" by two of his portraits.[2] Then after a hiatus of several years and moves to Chicago, Trenton again, Providence, and finally New York in 1858, he began to receive regular notice from newspaper critics, especially those in New York and Boston. His maturing style and his competence in both landscape and still life were recognized by the *Boston Transcript* in November 1859 when it commented: "Several flower pieces by Heade . . . are in drawing and coloring . . . remarkably truthful," while adding, "[He] has also on exhibition several quiet and accurate pictures of meadow scenery in Newburyport."[3]

One advantage of his frequent moves was that the critics of a given city often continued to view him as a local artist for years after he had gone. This was particularly true with Boston, where he lived for only two years (1861–63) but where his work was favorably reviewed by the *Transcript* and the *Evening Transcript* from September 1858 (when the former paper announced Heade's intention to live in Boston in the future), through the late 1870s.[4] In July 1860 the *Transcript* considered that "the pictures by Heade are probably the best he has ever exhibited"; while in October two marine views, one of which may have been *Seascape: Sunrise* (cat. 2), were much admired ("the huge waves as they curl and break upon the rocky shore are delineated with great truthfulness and feeling").[5] On the eve of Heade's departure for Brazil in 1863 the same paper called him "one of the best landscape painters of New England," and the following year — while Heade was abroad — it reported his progress on the hummingbird project and the honor he had received from the emperor of Brazil as a result of work he exhibited in Rio de Janeiro.[6] Over the years the Boston press continued to make favorable comments on the artist, in 1867, for example, opining that "none of our painters has a more refined sense of beauty or a more delicate feeling for color," and twenty years later admiring his latest Florida pictures: "There is a new picture here by Heade, a change from the usual stretch of marsh with late sunset; this time, a tropical swamp, dank, malarious, luxurious; palms and palmettos rising against a gorgeous sky; the execution is elaborate, the diffused light good."[7]

From the critics of New York, where Heade lived from 1858 to 1860, and again from 1866 to 1881, Heade also received frequent notices; their comments about his paintings were generally complimentary, though on occasion — especially as the years went on — they found fault with his work. He was favored with excellent reviews in 1859 and 1860, his first years in the city; one reviewer called his *Approaching Thunder Storm*, 1859 (cat. 1), at the National Academy of Design, "one of the best paintings in the exhibition" and added, "If Mr. Heade is capable of diverse statements of nature as true as this, he will make his mark."[8] A few months later, the important, short-lived journal the *Crayon* (which existed only from 1855 to 1861) remarked that his "occasional" still lifes were so "exquisite . . . that we are almost tempted to wish that he were less successful as a landscapist."[9] Similar approbation began to appear again after Heade's return to New York in mid-1866, and accolades appeared regularly in several papers there, including the *Evening Post*, the *Herald*, and the *Albion*. He was commended for "a very successful effect of sunset" and for a coastal scene "very truthfully drawn"; his *Mountains of Jamaica* was admired for the "marvellous power" with which the passing storm was painted; he was lauded for "a remarkably brilliant tropical scene," "an exquisite flower subject," and was singled out as "one of our most skillful flower painters."[10] The major critic of the 1850s and 1860s, Henry T. Tuckerman, also a resident of the Tenth Street Studio Building where Heade himself lived and a friend and admirer of Frederic E. Church and many other New York painters, devoted three complimentary paragraphs to Heade in his *Book of the Artists* of 1867. This was considerably less space than was given to discussions of Church, Albert Bierstadt, John F. Kensett, and several other members of the Hudson River School. However, Tuckerman knew those painters better and apparently liked and admired them more in personal terms than he did Heade, and we must not forget that whether or not an artist had a praiseworthy character — what critics were wont to describe as "sweetness," "generosity," or "nobility of character" — counted strongly among midcentury writers. Heade's personality was never described in such terms, and this in turn apparently affected the way in which his work was judged. Nonetheless, Tuckerman provided for Heade an accurate biographical summary, said that he "especially succeeds in representing marsh-lands . . . and the peculiar atmospheric effects thereof," praised his marine views ("where the effect of a thin overflow of water on the . . . beach is given with rare truth"), admired the small hummingbird pictures, and was especially enthusiastic about several still lifes of apple blossoms. Tuckerman concluded: "None of our painters has a more refined sense of beauty, or a more delicate feeling for color."[11]

At the same time, there were others who took a more jaundiced view of Heade's work. One of the most notable of this group was the collector-writer James Jackson Jarves, whose book of 1864 took a tack very different from Tuckerman's. Jarves was among the first to disparage the Hudson River School, whose work he found "realistic to a disagreeable degree"; he favored instead the newer, more idealizing landscape style represented by George Inness, Elihu Vedder, and John La Farge. He found Heade's marshes and seascapes "wearisome" but partially excepted him from his general condemnation of the school by virtue of his color, noting that his pictures were "flooded with rich sun-glow and sense of summer warmth."[12]

Jarves was an opponent of the school that Heade was aspiring to join, and his few words of criticism may not have been especially worrisome to the painter. However, during the 1860s other New York writers began to find fault with one aspect of Heade's work — his marine paintings — in specific and sometimes harsh terms, and this surely would have affected him. *Seascape: Sunset*, of 1861 (cat. 3), for example, was lauded by the *Boston Transcript* as "a work of uncommon merit, and enough to ensure the fame and success of any artist," but it was found wanting by the *New-York Daily Tribune*; the latter paper admired "the rich hue of the sky" but saw Heade's dark green water as "untrue" in its lack of any reflection of the red sky.[13] A few years later, Heade's large *Point Judith, Rhode Island*, 1867 (unlocated), was found by the *Round Table* to be "weak as to composition," and the following year the dramatic *Thunder Storm on Narragansett Bay*, 1868 (cat. 8), though attracting much attention, was treated severely by the *Brooklyn Daily Eagle*, which disliked the "unpleasant" yellow umbers, the "tiring" blacks, the weak flash of lightning, and the "inexplicable" light and shade. The critic concluded, "taken as a whole, the painting is very faulty."[14] To make matters worse, the same picture (which

played a key role in Heade's modern rediscovery, and which is now regarded as one of his greatest works) also received damning comments a few weeks later from another New York critic, T. C. Grannis, who disliked the picture's "hardness" and who wrote, "It is to be regretted that so hard and chilling a painting as this should have been allowed to leave his studio."[15] It is difficult to imagine a painter — especially one quite new to New York who was trying to compete with many long-established artists there — not being stung by these commentaries. Heade's immediate reaction, it would seem, was to give up making large, dramatic marine pictures, both the brilliant sunset views and the portentous thunderstorms, in favor of more benign renderings of landscape and still life. The New York criticism might also have reinforced in his mind the importance of maintaining the effective network he had built with dealers and exhibition officials in other cities.

Through the 1860s and 1870s the newspapers of New Haven, Philadelphia, San Francisco, Chicago, and the like would mention Heade — almost always admiringly — on occasion when his works were on view in those cities. The out-of-town critics were far less judgmental than their New York brethren, then as now, and the taste for the new French-oriented art moved west fairly slowly, so that Heade's brand of realism, which both public and press generally categorized with that of the Hudson River School, remained fashionable away from New York far longer than in that city. Moreover, the extent to which Heade had succeeded, by the end of his New York career, in becoming a popular, mainstream artist is suggested by an article that appeared in the May 1880 issue of *Scribner's Monthly*, entitled "The Young Painters of America." Defending the "new men" including La Farge, Inness, William Morris Hunt, and Winslow Homer, who aimed to "express feeling," the author cast Heade with painters such as Church and Kensett who had sought only to "imitate nature." The article disclaimed the old values, poking fun at critics who would say, " 'How true!' 'How life-like!' and 'How happily Mr. Heade has caught the hues of that hummingbird, and Mr. Eastman Johnson the attitude of that old man, and Mr. Brown the expression of that urchin.' "[16] Just the year before, another of the advanced critics, Clarence Cook, made the same points — about changing taste in art and Heade's established standing in the "old" school — when he complained that "there are scores of people who look at and admire Mr. Heade's picture while comparatively few either look at or admire Mr. [John Singer] Sargent's picture hung just beneath it." This struck the critic as ludicrous, given that Heade's *Tropical Flowers*, though "carefully painted," was in his view "not a work of art."[17]

As the tide of changing taste turned against him and the realist painters, Heade began his travels again, leaving New York for Washington, D.C., in the fall of 1881; during early 1883 he explored Florida and then settled in St. Augustine in March of that year. He lived and painted there for the rest of his life, patronized by the Standard Oil tycoon Henry Morrison Flagler and by numerous residents and winter visitors, respected as the dean of St. Augustine's art colony. His works were subject there only to praise from the local journals such as the *Tatler*; in its pages his northern marshes, his Florida scenes, his Brazilian orchids and passion flowers, along with the Cherokee roses and magnolias, all received unstinting admiration.

For a few years after he moved to Florida, Heade continued to send paintings to exhibitions in New York, Chicago, Louisville, Worcester, and Cincinnati, and to such dealers as Doll and Richards in Boston, James Earle in Philadelphia, and James D. Gill in Springfield, Massachusetts. After 1886, however, he shipped fewer and fewer works out of town, apparently finding enough patronage in St. Augustine itself to satisfy his needs. As taste changed and his works were rarely seen at exhibitions outside Florida, Heade was simply forgotten by the art establishment of the Northeast. He was granted a short paragraph in Clement and Hutton's *Artists of the Nineteenth Century* (1879), only a sentence in Samuel G. W. Benjamin's *Art in America* (1880), part of a sentence in Sarah Tytler's popular *Modern Painters and Their Paintings* (1874 and subsequent editions) and in Sadakichi Hartmann's *History of American Art* (1902), and not a word in the surveys that were written between Samuel Isham's *History of American Painting* (1905) and Edgar P. Richardson's *American Romantic Painting* (1944). Heade had simply been dropped from history.

His name was thus unknown to collectors and scholars alike when two New York dealers in early 1943 found *Thunder Storm on Narragansett Bay* in a Larchmont, New York, antique store and quickly sold it to a fortunate collector named Ernest Rosenfeld. The painting came to the attention of Dorothy Miller and James Thrall Soby, and they included it in their exhibition of the same year, *Romantic Painting in America*, at the Museum of Modern Art, where it caused a minor sensation. Quickly researching this new name, Miller discovered the outlines of Heade's biography, though she learned neither his life dates nor the fact of his late years in Florida. Soby's essay suggested that "the thunderous opera of the 1830 generation was nearing its end" (referring to Bierstadt and Thomas Moran) and considered Heade to be an example of "a quieter and more lyric Romantic landscape [that] was being evolved."[18] Thus, in a few sentences, Soby laid the groundwork for Barbara Novak's work a generation later.

Suddenly the search was on for paintings by the unknown

artist and for information about him. Boston's farsighted collector Maxim Karolik became a convert when he saw *Thunder Storm on Narragansett Bay* in the 1943 exhibition; too late to buy it, he pursued Heade's work avidly for years, buying some fifty works in the process. Several New York dealers took up the hunt, led by Harry Shaw Newman, Victor D. Spark, and Robert C. McIntyre of the Macbeth Gallery. In 1945 Newman commissioned the distinguished scholar Elizabeth McCausland to write an article about Heade, whom she described as "the artistic sensation of the 1943–44 season, when he reappeared to the art world."[19] The result was a fine, skeletal biography from his early life in Pennsylvania through the Florida years. McCausland, writing a half century ago, found most interesting in Heade's oeuvre the "fascinating iconography of humming birds and orchids which constitutes," she speculated, "his most potent esthetic appeal today."[20] Critics from that period up to our own have generally thought otherwise, and until recently more has been written about the coastal scenes and marshes than about Heade's flowers.

Also in 1945 Heade's work was included in the groundbreaking exhibition *The Hudson River School*, organized by Frederick Sweet, curator at the Art Institute of Chicago. Seen in both Chicago and New York, this show marked the start of the modern reappraisal of the landscape school.[21] In the same year Karolik presented the Museum of Fine Arts, Boston, with the great marine picture *Approaching Storm: Beach near Newport* (cat. 4), and shortly thereafter the Metropolitan Museum of Art, the Newark Museum, the Detroit Institute of Arts, and the Brooklyn Museum all acquired paintings by Heade. Until then, no American museum had actively sought his work.[22]

During the late forties, the dealer Robert C. McIntyre and John I. H. Baur, then curator at the Brooklyn Museum, began to investigate the painter. McIntyre's digging led to the discovery of numerous pictures and much biographical information and enabled him to write a remarkable book about Heade in 1948. Though McIntyre was untrained as an art historian, he laid out his findings in clear-cut fashion. Moreover, he was capable of both passion and eloquence, as is evident in his description of *Thunder Storm on Narragansett Bay*: "I was struck with the force of the thing, with the powerful drama being enacted — a sort of cosmic catastrophe, fraught with a breath-taking sense of elemental fury." He found in Heade's landscapes and seascapes special qualities of "atmosphere and mood" that distinguished him from his contemporaries; in all his work, but especially the orchids, he felt "a primeval and impressive loneliness."[23]

Baur, on the other hand, was a gifted young art historian with an interest in landscape painting and the Hudson River School that set him apart from other major scholars of this period. Playing off Jarves's dislike of the "coarse" pictures of the landscape school, Baur in his 1948 article, "Early Studies in Light and Air by American Landscape Painters," wrote of the artists' "concern with fleeting effects of atmosphere, with the momentary beauties of sunlight, mist or storm and with the transcription of light at specific times of day."[24] He found the "culmination" of this approach in the work of Fitz Hugh Lane, the Gloucester marine painter whose rediscovery during the twentieth century closely parallels Heade's, and in that of Heade himself. Like later writers, Baur struggled with the question of how much to differentiate "luminist" painting, as he called it, from the Hudson River School work. In one paragraph he points out the distinctions between them, noting that "romantic composition and a generally brown tonality" were typical of the Hudson River artists, but backtracking a moment

later when he described a keen interest in light in the work of Asher B. Durand and others. How to distinguish the Hudson River School from the luminists was a problem that would continue to vex scholars in this field.

Baur continued to work on Heade and Lane and the implication of their work in a series of articles over the next few years. His "Trends in American Painting, 1815-1865," the introduction to a scholarly catalogue of the Karolik collection, a pioneering publication of the Museum of Fine Arts in 1949, presented a thoughtful survey of midcentury painting, one that considers Heade and Lane together with their then better known contemporaries such as Kensett and Bierstadt.[25] In 1954 Baur continued his study of the phenomenon that he now christened "American Luminism" in an article of that title. He stressed that the term referred, not to "an organized movement," but rather to a group of "extreme realists" who were "the lyrical poets of the American countryside," and he distinguished them from the better-known artists of the Hudson River School whose works he found to be more painterly, both more panoramic and more romantic in compositional terms, and more "operatic." His two examples were Lane and Heade, and he perceptively distinguished between their styles, noting that Lane's work exceeded Heade's in its "polished and meticulous realism," while Heade's demonstrated a "greater concern with light and atmosphere."[26] Baur here concerned himself very little with Heade's floral paintings, a group of works then generally considered of less interest than the landscapes, but in another essay of the same year, this time an introduction to a traveling show of the Heades and Lanes in the Karolik Collection, he famously admired Heade's treatment of "the fleshy whiteness of magnolia blossoms startlingly arrayed on sumptuous red velvet like odalisques on a couch."[27]

Not everyone in the field shared in the excitement over Heade's work demonstrated by Karolik, McIntyre, and Baur. For example, Virgil Barker in his fine book of 1950, *American Painting*, dismisses Heade as "not a first-rate painter."[28] E. P. Richardson, whose *Painting in America* of 1956 is perhaps the best survey of the field written in these years, admired Heade as "an original, poetic observer," as seen in the orchid-and-hummingbird compositions, but had very little to say about the landscapes.[29] Along the same lines, Wolfgang Born in his studies of American still life (1947) and landscape (1948) preferred the tropical orchids as "the best of Heade's . . . work" and strangely found the "exactitude" of his sunsets and storms "more akin to the scientist than the romanticist."[30] Last of the survey writers of that generation, James T. Flexner handled Heade most sympathetically. In *That Wilder Image* of 1962 Flexner took a fresh look at the paintings and concluded that Heade's great works are those that employ high-value contrasts, sharply distinguished lights and darks — in other words, the reclining magnolias and the "eerie" thunderstorms at sea; he rated the more atmospheric marshes and orchids as secondary. This way of seeing Heade's work, rather than in the traditional categories of still life and landscape, offers interesting possibilities. In addition, Flexner also dealt briefly with the question of "luminism," perceptively suggesting that Baur's having grouped some of Kensett's pictures under this rubric "reveals that the movement was actually one aspect of the normal practice of the school Kensett led."[31]

This is, in a sense, where the first modern generation of historians of American art, led by Goodrich, Baur, Richardson, and Flexner, left off. They saw Heade as a more or less interesting artist of the second tier. There then entered the scene what might be called the "second generation" of Americanists, a

Fig. 18. *Coastal Scene with Sinking Ship*, 1863, oil on canvas. Shelburne Museum, Shelburne, Vermont, 27.1.4-58.

number of whom contributed to the study of Heade's work, including Barbara Novak, John Wilmerding, William H. Gerdts, and myself. It was a group of three Harvard graduate students (Gail Davidson, Phyllis Hattis, and I) who advanced the discussion next. In a brief exhibition catalogue of 1966 for the Fogg Art Museum entitled *Luminous Landscape: The American Study of Light, 1860–1875*, we proposed that luminism was a style inspired by Church and Lane and followed for a short time by some members of the Hudson River School, as the conventional Hudson River manner died out. Heade and Sanford R. Gifford were seen as the key practitioners, but we unaccountably neglected Kensett.[32] At the time, the concept of Luminism served a useful purpose, bringing together a group of important artists, who (except for Lane) knew one another well and whose work developed along similar lines in the 1850s and 1860s as they all demonstrated an increasing concern with light.

John Wilmerding's *History of American Marine Painting*, published in 1968 and the first study of its kind, found Heade to be of less interest than Lane as a marine painter, "but not a negligible artist." Wilmerding (perhaps thinking of Heade's marshes) suggested that the painter was "most at ease" with

Fig. 19. Fitz Hugh Lane (1804-1865), *Brace's Rock, Eastern Point, Gloucester,* 1863-64, oil on canvas. Private Collection.

small canvases "averaging twelve by twenty-four inches," but nonetheless found his major marine pictures to be three large-scale thunderstorms including *Coastal Scene with Sinking Ship*, 1863 (fig. 18), and the more famous ones in the collections at the Amon Carter Museum, Fort Worth, Texas (which purchased Ernest Rosenfeld's *Thunder Storm on Narragansett Bay* in 1977, cat. 8), and in the Karolik Collection at the Museum of Fine Arts, Boston (cat. 4). He also suggested that the "almost magical" similarity between Heade's *Stranded Boat* (cat. 7) and Lane's *Brace's Rock, Eastern Point, Gloucester* (fig. 19) points to Lane's influence on the younger painter.[33] This comparison would be taken up by several later writers, with mixed results.

With these works as prologue, the next few years found Heade for the first time widely viewed as a major painter, and they saw his work treated with increasing respect and sophistication by a variety of scholars. In 1969 William H. Gerdts and I organized the first retrospective exhibition that Heade's work had ever been accorded; it was seen at the University of Maryland Art Gallery, the Whitney Museum of American Art in New York, and the Museum of Fine Arts, Boston, and included fifty-one paintings along with drawings and prints. The catalogue essay expanded on McIntyre's biography, thanks to the many new paintings that had been found and the fact that more contemporary correspondence, exhibition records, and newspaper reviews had become available. It explored Heade's move to

Fig. 20. *Hummingbirds and Orchids*, about 1875-90, oil on canvas. The Detroit Institute of Arts, Founders Society Purchase, Dexter M. Ferry, Jr., Fund, 47.36.

New York in 1858, the stylistic distinctions between his work and that of Lane, Church, and the Hudson River School, his technique, his various series of paintings, and the sexual implications of his late still lifes. This exhibition and its catalogue, along with the reviews it engendered, had the effect of reintroducing Heade to scholars, collectors, and others interested in the field. The critics generally acclaimed Heade's rediscovery, John Canaday in the *New York Times*, for example, writing that the "conventions that he consistently observed hid from his contemporaries the extraordinary individualism of his interpretations,"[34] while the scholar Albert Boime enthused that "Heade was probably the most significant American painting landscapes in the nineteenth century."[35]

In 1970 the Metropolitan Museum of Art presented a grand exhibition entitled *19th-Century America: Paintings and Sculpture*, the first full-scale overview of the field since the Met's own *Life in America* of 1939. Whereas Heade had been omitted from the 1939 show, the new one included three of his paintings, the ubiquitous *Thunder Storm on Narragansett Bay*; *Spring Shower, Connecticut Valley* (now titled *April Showers*, cat. 21) from Boston; and *Hummingbirds and Orchids* (fig. 20), thus representing him as richly as Washington Allston, John Vanderlyn, Church, Bierstadt, and Homer, all long-acknowledged giants of our art.[36] The following year, William H. Gerdts provided the field with the first useful overview of our still-life tradition, including a discussion of

Heade's varied contributions to the genre over a forty-year period.[37] Gerdts was one of the few scholars studying American still life at this time; in general, the flood of interest in Heade that followed during the 1970s, in the form of dealer and museum exhibitions and publications, concentrated on Heade as a landscape painter.

In 1975 my own monograph on Heade was published. It apparently served a useful purpose in making available a far more complete picture of the artist than had hitherto existed. Included were an illustrated list of the 381 paintings then attributed to Heade, along with an account of his travels and his development as a painter of portraits, landscapes, and still lifes from 1839, the date of his first painting, to 1904, the time of his last work. I suggested stylistic sources and parallels for Heade's still lifes, including the orchids, and dealt also with the iconography of these works; I also added a cautionary note on luminism, on the potential usefulness of a more precise definition, and the limitations of an overly broad one.[38] I noted the scarcity of Heade's "minutes, letters, or conversation" and how little we knew of his life; fortunately, this is no longer true as recent research has brought to light a number of Heade's letters, his own Brazil/London journal, and many more contemporary reviews and exhibitions that included his work. In addition, the size of Heade's known oeuvre has risen by over 60 percent, as we now know about 620 paintings.

From all this increased evidence, it should be possible today to draw a richer and more complete picture of the artist than was possible before. Accordingly, our view of Heade's personality has been modified by what we have learned about his extensive network of friends, artists, dealers, and others, about his prolific output and the numerous places his work was exhibited each year. From what we now know, he surely was the loner he has long been described as being, one who charted his own course both on his travels and in his paintings, and he seems also to have been somewhat querulous and moody. However, we can no longer consider him a "misfit" or — given his public writings — "a humble, shy man," as I once described him.[39] Similarly, we must rethink some of the ways in which this painter has been described by other scholars, who with little evidence have surmised that he had "a tormented, contradictory personality"[40] and "a drinking problem,"[41] and that he projected in his landscapes "the severe psychological tensions and depths of a man who tagged along at the heels of the successful."[42]

It is not hard to see, in retrospect, how Heade came to be viewed as a tormented outsider. For one thing, he is rarely mentioned in the correspondence or the journals of his peers in New York, nor was he elected to the National Academy of Design or the Century Association, as were so many of his fellow painters. Other evidence was found in the paintings themselves: because they often evoke a mood of loneliness, occasionally even of despair, those qualities were easily moved from the art to the maker. Furthermore, Heade is known to have been outspoken politically, having publicly proclaimed his disgust with millionaires "who give a mere pittance now and then . . . while the poor are left to starve and freeze," then adding, "I am not likely to be placed in the ranks of 'boot lickers' to the rich."[43] His politics together with his constant moving and traveling made it easy for later scholars to think of him as an angry misfit. Thus the few available facts all seemed to point to Heade's being an isolated, romantic figure. This category, moreover, was much honored in American art history; the pioneering art historian Lloyd Goodrich did more than anyone else to establish it in the 1930s and 1940s by placing Homer,

Thomas Eakins, and Albert Pinkham Ryder — whom he saw as the trinity of native-born American greats — squarely within it. Heade's earliest biographer, Robert C. McIntyre, in his book of 1948, echoed Goodrich's nativist methodology while setting the tone for subsequent scholarship on this painter when he wrote: "Martin Heade was an individualist and a solitary, a creative artist as nearly independent of time and place as it is given to mortal man to become."[44] It takes nothing away from the excellence of McIntyre's book to add that while we still see Heade as an individualist, we no longer believe that he (or indeed almost any artist) can be truly "independent of time and place."

I believe that some of the greatest contributions made in this period, in terms of both the study of Heade and American painting in general, were made by Professor Barbara Novak. Her book of 1969, *American Painting of the Nineteenth Century*, challenged the field and raised discussion to a new level. Some of the proposals that Novak made have been subsequently amended, refined, or withdrawn, while others have won widespread acceptance; this was inevitable given her risky enterprise of trying to define a central style in eighteenth- and nineteenth-century American painting that could be explained in terms of this country's culture, philosophy, and literature, and the art itself. The structure of Novak's book was monographic, with twelve chapters on the painters whom she considered most significant, including Copley at the beginning, Homer, Eakins, and Ryder — the Goodrich trio of native American greats — at the end, and the newcomers Heade and Lane at the center of both the book and her argument. Luminism, which she defined as an "essentially conceptual vision, tempered by the primitive urge toward the clarity of the known and the bounded," was in her eyes "an indigenous mode of seeing,"

which most valued light, planar clarity, measurement, and the smallest facts of nature. Novak wrote that the luminist picture speaks spiritually of "the moment in Emerson's 'concentrated eternity.' "[45]

All this could be disputed, and was. Novak placed a heavy, selective burden on Emerson — too heavy, in the view of some scholars.[46] Church — whom David C. Huntington, as well as the authors of *Luminous Landscape*, had in 1966 proposed as the central figure in midcentury landscape painting — was inexplicably omitted. Some questioned whether luminism was properly "indigenous," and whether the concept arbitrarily omitted too much of a given artist's oeuvre, and too many whole oeuvres, from consideration.[47] Perhaps a little daunted, but unbowed, Novak in 1980 prepared a more sophisticated and more carefully reasoned sequel entitled *Nature and Culture: American Landscape and Painting, 1825–1875*. Luminism was still of major concern, but it was now given a smaller role, no longer being defined as the central American style, but rather as a notable manner in which some of the most interesting midcentury landscapists painted some of the time. Church entered from offstage to play a major part, not as luminism's founder, as Wilmerding and I had both theorized, but rather as the representative painter of "grand opera" (taking up an analogy originally suggested by Soby), as opposed to the "still small voice" of Heade and Lane. Luminism was explained — again reasonably — as a new "sublime" with roots in the work of Thomas Cole and Henry David Thoreau. The history of science and especially the writings of Charles Darwin were usefully introduced; Novak analyzed the meaning and background of Darwin's *On the Origin of Species* (1859) thoroughly but concluded that "Darwin came . . . too late to upset the reverential tone" that characterizes American landscape painting.[48] Subsequent writers have disagreed on the latter point. Stephen Jay Gould in his important essay on Church in 1989, for example, traced the loss of conviction one sees in that painter's work after the mid-1860s to changing attitudes represented by rapid acceptance of Darwin's theories.[49] Gould speculates that the "collapse" of Church's vision, represented by the replacing of Humboldt's worldview with Darwin's, made it impossible for Church (or by implication anyone else) ever to paint such landscapes again.

Novak's work has had significant effects. By reaching deeply into American culture to seek sources and analogues for the paintings, she opened up discourse with scholars in other fields who in turn have employed their own methodologies in enriching the discussion. Robert Rosenblum, the well-known scholar of European art, in his key book of 1975, *Modern Painting and the Northern Romantic Tradition*, situates Heade's paintings of orchids within the Northern Romantic tradition, relating him to both Robert John Thornton (the British naturalist) and Van Gogh.[50] In 1976 the Museum of Modern Art in *The Natural Paradise* exhibition again championed Heade's work when thirteen of his paintings were boldly exhibited alongside those of Church and Kensett, on the one hand, and of Jackson Pollock, Barnett Newman, and the New York School of a century later, on the other. In his essay there, Rosenblum compared Mark Rothko's "special fusion of lambent color and atmospheric expansiveness" with the "silent, primordial void of light and space" one finds in Heade's work.[51]

If the enthusiasm on the part of modernists for Heade and his contemporaries was relatively short-lived, the interest that Novak, Wilmerding, and others sparked among students of American culture has proved to be both long-lasting and significant. For example, two articles on Thoreau and luminism appeared in 1980, one by John Conron, the other by Barton Levi St. Armand, and both made excellent contributions. Conron skillfully tied an analysis of luminist paintings to Thoreau's "travel account," *A Week on the Concord and Merrimack Rivers*, describing the ways that the structure of the book (including "its progress outward from the river and the valley into a universe of light and air"), its seven chapters (each beginning "with an evocation of the morning light," each ending by describing twilight), and certain individual passages, brings to mind the work of Heade and Lane.[52] St. Armand, like Conron, begins with Baur and Novak, while also citing the latter's tendency to "undisciplined overstatement" in her 1969 book. He then describes Thoreau's concern with "multiple strata of reflection and the ever-changing effect of light" and "shifting atmospheric phenomena" at Walden Pond and finds his technique similar to Heade's, in that each observed a single marsh for long periods, under varying conditions. St. Armand effectively brings specific paintings together with passages from Thoreau, as when he finds numerous methodological parallels between Heade's *Approaching Storm: Beach near Newport* (cat. 4) and *Cape Cod* by Thoreau.[53] As one sees in both of these articles, for scholars, and especially for the non–art historians, Heade and Lane were now considered the archetypal luminists, and one rarely reads of Kensett, Gifford, or the others in their writings.

It was a doctoral thesis by a student of Novak's at Columbia University that brought Heade's still lifes back into the discussion and that suggested a new context in which to see them. The work was Ella M. Foshay's *Nineteenth-Century American Flower Painting and the Botanical Sciences* (1979), the whole of which is available only in a printed-microfilm form.[54] Foshay postulates that as botanical theories changed from Linnaeus to Darwin, so did the mind-set of the American flower painter. Pre-Darwinian artists are seen as aiming to depict flowers' "unchanging perfection of design and God-given beauty"[55] with scientific accuracy, while post-Darwinian artists including Heade presented "a dynamic and integrated view of nature,"[56] one emphasizing the "principles of physiological growth and the integral relationship of the growing flower to its surroundings."[57] These qualities come directly, Foshay writes, from the speedy, widespread acceptance of Darwin's landmark book, *On the Origin of Species*. Heade's paintings, frequently picturing two fighting hummingbirds (illustrating Darwin's "war of nature") together with living, flowering plants reeking of growth and decay, from which they could feed or pollinate, she sees as perfect illustrations of Darwin.[58] Novak, we recall, clearly outlined the Darwinian revolution in America in *Nature and Culture*, published in 1980, but stopped short of seeing anything of Darwin's influence in the work of Heade or any of the luminists.[59]

Other scholars have extended Foshay's argument. The new worldview implied by *On the Origin of Species* is now considered one of the major factors for the change of style that occurred in our painting during the 1860s and 1870s.[60] One scholar, Katherine Manthorne, carefully examined Heade's place in the great debate of the 1860s, which pitted the old "creationist" views of Alexander von Humboldt and Louis Agassiz against the new ones propagated by Darwin. She found that the dramatic changes that take place in Heade's depictions of hummingbirds between the mid-1860s and early 1870s (the development from the close-up portraiture of *The Gems of Brazil* to the natural integration of birds, flowers, and tropical landscape in the orchid and passion flower pictures) "closely parallel the direction of Darwin's researches, which were replacing a static

view of nature with a perception of the organic world as a dynamic and interrelated system."[61] Regarding Heade's orchid-and-hummingbird paintings, Manthorne writes: "There is a visionary aura about these pictures . . . that suggests the almost Gothic anxiety the artist felt in the face of the crisis precipitated by Darwin."[62] Finally, it is worth noting that the views of Foshay and Manthorne were given important though indirect support by Harvard's distinguished scientist Stephen Jay Gould, in his important article of 1989 cited above.

Heade's stature continued to rise through the eighties and nineties. The much-acclaimed exhibition *American Light: The Luminist Movement, 1850–1875*, organized by John Wilmerding for the National Gallery of Art, included nineteen works by Heade, making him one of the four best-represented artists.[63] The *New World* exhibition, which in 1983–84 introduced Paris to nineteenth-century American painting, represented Heade as one of the dozen or so "major" artists at work in this country between the mid-eighteenth and early twentieth centuries.[64] Finally, in the Metropolitan Museum's *American Paradise: The World of the Hudson River School* (1989), the most recent broad-reaching exhibition of nineteenth-century painting, Heade was again ranked as a highly significant figure. Seven of his paintings were included there, making him one of the best-represented "Hudson River School" painters, though other scholars — myself included — have increasingly come to doubt that Heade is most usefully seen as standing within that school. It should be added that the essays in *American Paradise*, on the historiography of the school by Kevin J. Avery, on its style by Oswaldo Rodriguez Roque, on the market environment by John K. Howat, and on the decline of the style by Doreen Bolger and Catherine Hoover Voorsanger, offer a good survey of the American landscape school.[65]

Fig. 21. *Rio de Janeiro Bay*, 1864, oil on canvas. National Gallery of Art, Washington, D.C., Gift of the Avalon Foundation, 1965.2.1.

Franklin Kelly has made several recent contributions to the Heade literature. In the National Gallery of Art catalogue of the private collection of Richard Manoogian — the greatest Heade enthusiast since Karolik — Kelly's entries on Heade are particularly insightful in their discussion of the complex questions surrounding Heade's *Gems of Brazil* project from the mid-1860s.[66] Then in 1996 Kelly and his colleagues produced that rarity, a catalogue of a museum's permanent collection that advances — rather than merely reiterates — scholarship.[67] The National Gallery had fallen behind other major museums in collecting Heade's work, having for years only one rather atypical example, *Rio de Janeiro Bay* (fig. 21), but in recent years has purchased an outstanding orchid-and-hum-

mingbird picture (cat. 57) as well as one of the most beautiful of all the painter's late still lifes, *Giant Magnolias on a Blue Velvet Cloth* (cat. 71), in 1996.

Timothy A. Eaton has made two useful additions to the Heade literature. First, in 1992 he organized a touring exhibition with a richly illustrated catalogue of twenty-four oil sketches by Heade owned by the St. Augustine Historical Society.[68] This publication served to remind us, once again, of how different Heade was from his major contemporaries. Where the Hudson River School painters, especially Church, made numerous oil sketches of landscape subjects, Heade executed almost none. Instead, nearly alone among American painters, he made a series of such sketches of roses, orchids, magnolias, and other favorite flowers, studies he kept all his life and that he used over and over again in his finished compositions. Second, in 1996 Eaton organized a small survey of all aspects of Heade's work from his early days in Bucks County to his late years in Florida. The catalogue for this exhibition includes another look at the painter by Barbara Novak. In an eloquent, thoughtful essay, Novak turns her attention for the first time to Heade's personality and to his flower paintings, which she found "intense, daring, original . . . unabashedly sensual." The author there continued to find Heade's marshes luminist and Emersonian, and even as she allowed that his orchids contain "Darwinian energies" she concluded that many different readings of these complex works may be valid.[69]

Investigation of Heade's favorite subject, the marsh, has lagged behind the attention given to his seascapes and still lifes and to the concept of "luminism" in his work. In 1975 I suggested how unlike normal Hudson River School pictures the marshes are, how they represented an in-between subject — neither wilderness nor farm — that became Heade's Walden.[70] Bruce Johnson, in his thoughtful article of 1980, qualified Novak's argument in her *Nature and Culture* of earlier that year, arguing that Heade's Huck Finn–like individualism distinguishes his marsh scenes from both the Hudson River School and from much of "luminism" as Novak defines it.[71] Johnson finds in these works a "repose" that is primarily symbolic of a "measured and disciplined watching and waiting" that stands apart from any relationship to manifest destiny, a Christian sublime, or even the mystical transcendentalism suggested by Novak. In his 1989 book, *Dark Eden*, David C. Miller explored the question of the marshes from a different angle, in the process putting Heade's love of these subjects into cultural context. He tells us that in this period "Americans began turning to new landscapes to express their changing perceptions of nature" and that the choice of these "previously neglected" swamps, marshes, tropical forests, and the like reflected a "deep-seated cultural strain" in the Civil War era. In painting marshes and swamps from Massachusetts to Florida, Heade took on a subject long thought to be unhealthy, one wholly lacking in the picturesque, allegorical, romantic qualities that Church and the Hudson River School had valued so highly. Miller persuasively outlines the implications of what he describes as "the transition from a primarily moral relationship to nature to one that is largely psychological," and thus enables us to understand Heade's accomplishment more fully.[72]

During the last decade, several able scholars have given renewed attention to Heade's marine subjects, dealing particularly with the thunderstorm pictures that lay at the heart of the Heade revival in 1943–45. J. Gray Sweeney in 1988 aimed at an "in-depth analysis" of *Thunder Storm on Narragansett Bay* without the baggage of previous writers' "formalist and/or existentialist concerns."[73] Pointing out that the memory of Thomas Cole was alive at the time Heade was at work (the twentieth anniversary of his death being 1868), Sweeney draws our attention to the formal similarities between the calm, black water in Heade's *Thunder Storm on Narragansett Bay* and Cole's *Voyage of Life: Old Age* (fig. 22), an idea first put forth by Roger Stein in 1975,[74] and suggests, not unreasonably, an echo of Cole's whole series in Heade's picture. Overall, he found the painting to carry a "singularly unrelieved tenor of pessimism." He points out also the skeletal remains of a ship at the center foreground in Heade's composition, as well as such details as the broken-down fence at the left, which he sees as one of two Christian crosses in this area, and just below it a grimacing rock and a "swelling form," which he believes "suggests a human body beneath the sands." Sweeney's argument is weakened by such overreading of the painting. Many

Fig. 22. Thomas Cole (1801–1848), *The Voyage of Life: Old Age*, 1842, oil on canvas. Munson-Williams-Proctor Institute Museum of Art, Utica, New York, 55.108.

observers do not read every detail as he does, but the article does serve to remind us of Cole's influence on the next generation of painters, and it compels us to inquire after the "richer and more complex meanings" in Heade's work that may have been overlooked.

David Miller's article on the iconology of wrecked and stranded boats in nineteenth-century American painting contains numerous insights, despite being based on several visual comparisons that fail, I believe, to be entirely convincing.[75] Thus, Miller makes a good deal out of contrasting a stormy marine composition by the eighteenth-century French painter Claude-Joseph Vernet with a calm, luminous view of a quiet coastline by an American of the next century, Francis A. Silva: where Miller finds a European sensibility in the Vernet and a specifically American "mood of aftermath" in the Silva, others might find that the comparison tells us more about the eighteenth-century mind versus that of the nineteenth century, with questions of nationality being peripheral. Miller goes on to compare Heade's *Stranded Boat*, 1863 (cat. 7) — now a famous painting — with Lane's *Brace's Rock* of 1864 in the Terra Foundation Collection (Lane executed at least four versions of the same subject, all of the same size, in 1863–64), a comparison Wilmerding and Novak had both made years before (see fig. 19). If the pairing of these works made an interesting point in earlier years, when defining luminism was of primary interest, it seems less useful today as we come to realize how very different the two painters were. Lane's paintings of Brace's Rock are everything Novak and Miller suggest, tightly concentrated works of high gloss and keen realism that are both minimal and moral, paintings whose tight skins make the viewer's entry impossible. Heade's *Stranded Boat*, on the other hand, suggests a different kind of narrative. If *Brace's Rock* is an "epiphany," then *The Stranded Boat* (its misleading title given by a long-forgotten dealer or curator) speaks to time and the stages of man's life: in it one sees a distant boat emerging from a fog, another that is closer, then a third that has been carefully secured on the beach, its sail furled and the oars stowed (this working craft belongs to a skilled mariner), while the sailor himself or a compatriot has walked far out on a rocky point to survey the sea — or perhaps his destiny — again. Lane is a painter of light, while Heade portrayed weather and atmosphere, the coming or lifting of fog or rain, and the slow, palpable changes in the sky and on the earth. If we continue to label both artists as luminists, it may be at the expense of understanding both the similarities and the differences in their work.

Miller's article is nonetheless praiseworthy. He makes brilliant use of the decayed boat that Thoreau describes in *Walden*, especially in his parallel consideration of Worthington Whittredge's *Old Hunting Grounds* of about 1864 (fig. 23), a vertical, nonluminist woodland scene of a kind that is generally ignored in today's scholarship. He ties the cultural and visual changes he surveys to Darwin, among others, and he concludes with a discussion of the profound ways in which "the heroically conceived visions that had dominated the American

Fig. 23. Worthington Whittredge (1820–1910), *The Old Hunting Grounds*, about 1864, oil on canvas. Reynolda House, Museum of American Art, Winston-Salem, North Carolina.

landscape tradition through the Civil War" unraveled, adding that in the literature and the paintings (especially those of Heade), "human history, with its tacit assumptions, dogma, and teleology, is supplanted by natural history, with its endlessly repetitive cycles and rhythms."[76]

Sarah Cash is the latest scholar to contribute to the discussion. Again concentrating on Heade's marine and shoreline views, she was one of the first to make a careful study of some of the sites where he worked. In the process, she has proven that several of his most admired works, long thought to portray the coast at Newport, Rhode Island, actually depict Singing Beach at Manchester, Massachusetts, on Boston's North Shore.[77] More significant, she took on one of the painter's archetypal works, *Thunder Storm on Narragansett Bay*, in an effort to put it into the context of Heade's oeuvre and his times. Through some fine research, Cash discovered that Heade's two earliest thunderstorm-over-water pictures were owned originally by prominent nineteenth-century preachers, Henry Ward Beecher and Noah Hunt Schenck, both of whom frequently employed thunderstorm and endangered-ship-of-state imagery in their sermons of the Civil War era.[78] All this is unarguable, but Cash appears to overreach in drawing the conclusions she does from her evidence. She finds that Schenck's rhetoric in the pulpit "leaves little doubt as to his thoughts when he contemplated [Heade's] *Approaching Thunder Storm*," and says, "it is certain that at least the collectors . . . and his fellow creators . . . believed that the subject [Heade] chose was laden with contemporary meaning . . . at a very specific and traumatic point in the country's history [e.g., the Civil War]."[79] With regard to Beecher, who owned another marine of 1859, she never asks why, if Beecher wanted to own paintings that reflected his thoughts, none of the other seventy-five pictures he owned in 1863 apparently depicted either a storm or a Civil War scene.[80] One also wonders whether her interpretation would apply to all of the stormy landscapes and marines painted in America during the war, as well as long before and well after it. Moreover, Beecher's sermon of 1859,

"The Storm and Its Lessons" — which Cash cites — does not speak of "the impending doom of war" at all, but rather concludes: "If we had had no experience, I can not imagine any thing more shocking than a summer storm. It is because we have outlived so many that we do not fear them."[81] As John Updike astutely wrote in response to Cash's thesis, "Studying the set of storm paintings, I could not bring myself to believe that they had much to do with the Civil War and Reconstruction."[82]

Few American painters have received more critical attention than Heade during the past twenty-five years. As we have seen, he was generally considered a marginal figure during his lifetime, and for years after his death his name was simply unknown to historians. Yet recent critics and collectors have found his work compelling in its originality; we are fascinated by the ways it relates to yet differs from the paintings of his contemporaries. Nineteenth-century critics found fault with Heade's pictures because of their harshness, their repetitiveness, their lack of topographical interest; now we value them for exactly these same qualities, as well as for the way his different series seem to have been conceived and executed in an almost modern way. Today we admire the subtlety of his atmospheric effects, the glory of his light, the sumptuous warmth of the orchids and tropical scenes, and the inexplicable sensuality of so many of his works in every genre. Above all, to our eyes Heade's work seems wonderfully rich in its handling, its iconography, its originality, and its meaning. We can only wonder what his reaction might be to find his paintings being exhibited in 1999–2000 on a nationwide tour to three of this country's great museums.

THEODORE E. STEBBINS, JR.

1. See Henry T. Tuckerman, *Book of the Artists* (New York: G. P. Putnam and Sons, 1867; New York: James L. Carr, 1967), and James Jackson Jarves, *The Art-Idea* (New York: Hurd & Houghton, 1864; Cambridge, Mass.: Belknap Press, 1960).

2. [Junior Editor], "Fine Arts," *Western Journal and Civilian* 7 (October 1851), p. 73.

3. "Art Items," *Boston Transcript*, November 1, 1859, p. 2. In gathering information on both newspaper reviews that mention Heade and exhibitions that included his work, I have received immeasurable assistance from Prof. William H. Gerdts, Merl M. Moore, Jr., and Alfred Harrison, for which I am profoundly grateful.

4. "Art Intelligence," *Boston Transcript*, September 22, 1858, p. 2.

5. "Art Matters," *Boston Transcript*, July 27, 1860, p. 2; "Art Items," *Boston Transcript*, October 20, 1860, p. 4.

6. "Art Enterprise," *Boston Transcript*, August 12, 1863, p. 2; "An American Artist Decorated," *Boston Transcript*, August 12, 1864, p. 2.

7. *Boston Daily Evening Transcript*, July 1, 1867, p. 2; "Art Notes: Things in the Summer Hangings of the Galleries," *Boston Daily Evening Transcript*, August 21, 1885, p. 4.

8. "National Academy of Design: Fourth Gallery," *Home Journal* (New York), May 5, 1860, p. 2.

9. "Sketchings," *Crayon* 7, no. 9 (September 1860), p. 264.

10. "a very successful effect of sunset": "Fine Arts. The Artists' Fund Exhibition. (Second Notice)," *Albion*, November 24, 1866, p. 561; "very truthfully drawn": "Art in the Union League Club," *New York Evening Post*, February 12, 1869, p. 2; "marvellous power": "A New Tropical Landscape," *New York Evening Post*, September 10, 1870, p. 2; "a remarkably brilliant tropical scene": "Art Notes," *New York Evening Post*, January 4, 1872, p. 1; "an exquisite flower subject": "Art Notes," *New York Evening Post*, October 8, 1872, p. 1; "one of our most skillful flower painters": "Mr. Schenck's Art Gallery," *New York Evening Post*, March 21, 1876, p. 3.

11. Tuckerman, *Book of the Artists*, pp. 542–543.

12. Jarves, *The Art-Idea*, p. 193.

13. "Art Items," *Boston Transcript*, February 27, 1861, p. 2; *New-York Daily Tribune*, March 27, 1861, p. 8.

14. "Pictures at the National Academy," *Round Table*, May 18, 1867, p. 310; "The Art Association: Third Day of the Exhibition — More of the Pictures," *Brooklyn Daily Eagle*, March 21, 1868, p. 2.

15. T. C. Grannis, *National Academy of Design: Exhibition of 1868* (New York, 1868), p. 87. It should be noted that the New York critics were occasionally also hard on Heade's other works: for example, in October 1870, the *New York Evening Mail* wrote that Heade's *Mountains of Jamaica* was "a weak monotonous wash of color, uninteresting to the last degree" ("Art Gossip," October 25, 1870, p. 1).

16. "The Younger Painters of America," *Scribner's Monthly* 20, no. 1 (May 1880), p. 7.

17. [Clarence Cook], "Academy of Design: Fifty-fourth Annual Exhibition," *New-York Daily Tribune*, April 26, 1879, p. 5.

18. James Thrall Soby, "Romantic Painting in America," in James Thrall Soby and Dorothy C. Miller, *Romantic Painting in America*, exh. cat. (New York: The Museum of Modern Art, 1943), p. 20.

19. Elizabeth McCausland, "Martin Johnson Heade, 1819–1904," *Panorama* 1, no. 1 (October 1945), p. 4.

20. Ibid., p. 5.

21. Frederick K. Sweet, *The Hudson River School and the Early American Landscape Tradition*, exh. cat. (Chicago: The Art Institute of Chicago, 1945).

22. The Metropolitan Museum of Art purchased *Jersey Meadows with Ruins of a Haycart* in 1945; the Detroit Institute of Arts received the gift of two Heades, *Sunset* (a marsh scene) and *Hummingbirds and Orchids* (fig. 20) from Dexter M. Ferry, Jr., in 1946 and 1947, respectively; the Newark Museum purchased *Jersey Meadows with a Fisherman* in 1946; and the Brooklyn Museum purchased *Summer Showers* (cat. 10) in 1947.

23. Robert G. McIntyre, *Martin Johnson Heade* (New York: Pantheon Press, 1948), pp. 2, 43, 45.

24. John I. H. Baur, "Early Studies in Light and Air by American Landscape Painters," *Brooklyn Museum Bulletin* 9 (winter 1948), p. 1.

25. John I. H. Baur, "Trends in American Painting, 1815-1865," *M. and M. Karolik Collection of American Paintings, 1815–1865* (Cambridge, Mass.: Harvard University Press, 1949), pp. xv-lvii.

26. John I. H. Baur, "American Luminism," *Perspectives USA* 9 (Autumn 1954), pp. 90-94.

27. John I. H. Baur, Introduction, *Commemorative Exhibition: Paintings by Martin J. Heade (1819–1904), Fitz Hugh Lane (1804–1865) from the Private Collection of Maxim Karolik and the M. and M. Karolik Collection of American Paintings from the Museum of Fine Arts, Boston*, exh. cat. (New York: M. Knoedler and Company, 1954).

28. Virgil Barker, *American Painting: History and Interpretation* (New York: Macmillan, 1950), p. 419.

29. E. P. Richardson, *Painting in America: The Story of 450 Years* (New York: Crowell, 1956), p. 227.

30. Wolfgang Born, *Still-Life Painting in America* (New York: Oxford University Press, 1947), p. 29; Born, *American Landscape Painting* (New Haven, Conn.: Yale University Press, 1948), p. 69.

31. James Thomas Flexner, *That Wilder Image: The Paintings of America's Native School from Thomas Cole to Winslow Homer* (Boston: Bonanza, 1962), p. 280.

32. Gail Davidson, Phyllis Hattis, Theodore E. Stebbins, Jr., *Luminous Landscape: The American Study of Light, 1860-1875*, exh. cat. (Cambridge, Mass.: Fogg Art Museum, Harvard University, 1966).

33. John Wilmerding, *A History of American Marine Painting* (Salem, Mass.: Peabody Museum, 1968), pp. 177, 182; see also Wilmerding, *American Art* (New York: Penguin, 1976), pp. 96-97 for a good summary of Heade's career with an emphasis on his role as a luminist and on the connection between his work and Lane's. Wilmerding in his *Fitz Hugh Lane* (New York: Praeger, 1971), pp. 84-85, also posited Heade's possible influence on Lane at the same time, pointing to Lane's *Riverdale* (1863, Cape Ann Historical Association, Gloucester, Mass.) and its similarity to such Heade paintings as *Sunrise on the Marshes* (cat. 12).

34. John Canaday, "M. J. Heade: American Loner," *New York Times*, November 16, 1969, p. 25.

35. Albert Boime, "New York: A Landscapist for All Seasons and Dr. Jekyll and Martin Heade," *Burlington Magazine* 112, no. 803 (February 1970), p. 127.

36. John K. Howat et al., *19th-Century America: Paintings and Sculpture*, exh. cat. (New York: The Metropolitan Museum of Art, 1970), cat. nos. 139-141.

37. William H. Gerdts and Russell Burke, *American Still Life Painting* (New York: Praeger, 1971); see also William H. Gerdts, *Painters of the Humble Truth: Masterpieces of American Still Life, 1801–1839* (Columbia: University of Missouri Press, 1981).

38. Theodore E. Stebbins, Jr., *The Life and Works of Martin Johnson Heade* (New Haven, Conn.: Yale University Press, 1975).

39. Theodore E. Stebbins, Jr., *Martin Johnson Heade*, exh. cat. (College Park: University of Maryland Art Gallery, 1969), unpaginated.

40. Boime, "A Landscapist for All Seasons," p. 127.

41. J. Gray Sweeney, "A 'very peculiar' Picture: Martin J. Heade's *Thunderstorm over Narragansett Bay*," *Archives of American Art Journal* 28, no. 4 (1988), p. 7.

42. Bruce Johnson, "Martin Johnson Heade's Salt Marshes and the American Sublime," *Porticus: The Journal of the Memorial Art Gallery of the University of Rochester* 3 (1980), p. 36.

43. Didymus [Martin Johnson Heade], "Game Parks and Other Things," *Forest and Stream* 60 (February 7, 1903), p. 108; Didymus, "Game Parks Again," *Forest and Stream* 60 (April 4, 1903), p. 268.

44. McIntyre, *Martin Johnson Heade*, p. 42.

45. Barbara Novak, *American Paintings of the Nineteenth Century* (New York: Praeger, 1969), pp. 23, 125, 105.

46. Gayle L. Smith, "Emerson and the Luminist Painters: A Study of Their Styles," *American Quarterly* 37, no. 2 (summer 1985), pp. 193-215.

47. See William H. Gerdts, *American Luminism*, exh. cat. (New York: Coe Kerr Gallery, 1978). In one of the most thoughtful essays to be written about "luminism," Gerdts cautions that "parallel developments evocative of luminism can be discovered to varying degrees in the art of other nations," and he then briefly describes a number of such parallels in German, Danish, Russian, English, and Italian landscape painting. Both Barbara Novak and I, unbeknownst to each other, in 1980 responded by preparing essays on this subject which contain many similarities. Hers appeared as chapter 10, "America and Europe: Influence and Affinity," in her book *Nature and Culture: American Landscape and Painting, 1825–1875* (New York: Oxford University Press, 1980), pp. 226-273; mine is "Luminism in Context: A New View" in John Wilmerding et al., *American Light: The Luminist Movement, 1850–1875*, exh. cat. (Washington, D.C.: National Gallery of Art, 1980), pp. 211-234. For a well-reasoned, critical consideration of "luminism," see Andrew Wilton, "American Light: The Luminist Movement," in *Burlington Magazine*, October 1980, pp. 715-716.

48. Novak, *Nature and Culture,* p. 76.

49. Stephen Jay Gould, "Church, Humboldt, and Darwin: The Tension and Harmony of Art and Science," in Franklin Kelly et al., *Frederic Edwin Church*, exh. cat. (Washington, D.C.: National Gallery of Art, 1989), pp. 94ff.

50. Robert Rosenblum, *Modern Painting and the Northern Romantic Tradition: Friedrich to Rothko* (New York: Harper & Row, 1975), pp. 82-83.

51. Robert Rosenblum, "The Primal American Scene," in Kynaston McShine, ed., *The Natural Paradise: Painting in America, 1800–1950*, exh. cat. (New York: The Museum of Modern Art, 1976), pp. 18-22.

52. John Conron, " 'Bright American Rivers': The Luminist Landscapes of Thoreau's *A Week on the Concord and Merrimack Rivers*," *American Quarterly* 32, no. 2 (summer 1980), pp. 151, 161. See also Kevin Radaker, " 'A Separate Intention of the Eye': Luminist Eternity in Thoreau's *A Week on the Concord and Merrimack Rivers*," *Canadian Review of American Studies* 18, no. 1 (spring 1987), pp. 41-60. For Walt Whitman as luminist, see Stephen Adams, "The Luminist Walt Whitman," *American Poetry* 2, no. 2 (winter 1985), pp. 2-16.

53. Barton Levi St. Armand, "Luminism in the Work of Henry David Thoreau: The Dark and the Light," *Canadian Review of American Studies* 11, no. 1 (spring 1980), pp. 15-16. See also the salutary article by Gayle L. Smith, "Emerson and the Luminist Painters: A Study of Their Styles" (as in n. 46). In her excellent analysis of the ways that Emerson's work can and cannot be compared to luminist paintings, Smith writes: "The art critics tend, quite naturally, to focus on what is most quotable in Emerson, frequently taking statements out of context" (p. 194).

54. Ella Milbank Foshay, *Nineteenth-Century American Flower Painting and the Botanical Sciences*, Ph.D. diss., Columbia University, 1979 (Ann Arbor, Mich.: UMI Research Press, 1981); see also Foshay, "Charles Darwin and the Development of American Flower Imagery," *Winterthur Portfolio* (winter 1980), pp. 299-314, which briefly summarizes the thesis; also Foshay, *Reflections of Nature: Flowers in American Art*, exh. cat. (New York: Whitney Museum of American Art, 1984).

55. Foshay, *Reflections of Nature*, p. 36.

56. Ibid., p. 52.

57. Foshay, *Nineteenth-Century American Flower Painting*, p. 215.

58. Ibid.

59. Novak has continued to refine her theory in recent years. In her introduction to Barbara Novak et al., *The Thyssen-Bornemisza Collection: Nineteenth-Century American Painting* (New York: The Vendome Press, 1986), she makes more modest claims for luminism, writing: "Though pure luminism is rare, luminist passages, luminist mood, luminist glow abound in American

painting." She continues: "The purest luminist paintings were produced most consistently by Lane and Heade and to a lesser extent by Hudson River men such as Kensett and, on occasion, Gifford" (p. 28). Novak sees these painters as unaffected by Darwinism, concluding: "The stable infinity in which luminism has its being is the perfect expositor of the pre-Darwinian concept of Design. Everything is in its place. . . . Immutable as species, forms reside within their platonic envelopes" (p. 29). See also Novak's 1995 Preface to the second edition of her *Nature and Culture*, an excellent discourse on possible ways that some of the new methodologies in art history — for example, ones that aim to "resituate" the text (e.g., works of art) in "the sociopolitical and economic sites of its production" (Novak here quotes Giles Gunn, *Thinking across the American Grain: Ideology, Intellect, and the New Pragmatism* [Chicago: University of Chicago Press, 1992], p. 167) — can be reconciled with more traditional formalist, aesthetic, and iconographic analysis. Here she again maintained that the luminists were by definition not subject to what she described as "the post-Darwinian crisis of faith" (p. xvi).

60. See, for example, the excellent essay on the Hudson River School, Oswaldo Rodriguez Roque, "The Exaltation of American Landscape Painting," in John K. Howat et al., *American Paradise: The World of the Hudson River School*, exh. cat. (New York: The Metropolitan Museum of Art, 1987), which concludes that: "The ideas that had been at the core of the entire Hudson River School tradition lost their immediacy as they confronted, first, a new Darwinian science . . . and, second, a new mood in the country, which after the horrors of the Civil War could no longer perceive of itself as the new Eden" (p. 48).

61. Katherine Emma Manthorne, *Tropical Renaissance: North American Artists Exploring Latin America, 1839–1879* (Washington, D.C., and London: Smithsonian Institution Press, 1989), p. 127. Manthorne credits Ella M. Foshay with originating this interpretation.

62. Manthorne, *Tropical Renaissance*, p. 130.

63. Wilmerding et al., *American Light*.

64. Theodore E. Stebbins, Jr., Carol Troyen, and Trevor J. Fairbrother, *A New World: Masterpieces of American Painting, 1760–1910*, exh. cat. (Boston: Museum of Fine Arts, Boston, 1983).

65. Howat et al., *American Paradise*.

66. *American Paintings from the Manoogian Collection*, exh. cat. (Washington, D.C.: National Gallery of Art, 1989).

67. Franklin Kelly et al., *American Paintings of the Nineteenth Century, Part I* (Washington, D.C.: National Gallery of Art, 1996).

68. Timothy A. Eaton, ed., *Martin Johnson Heade: The Floral and Hummingbird Studies from the St. Augustine Historical Society*, exh. cat. (Boca Raton, Fla.: Boca Raton Museum of Art, 1992).

69. Barbara Novak, *Martin Johnson Heade: A Survey, 1840–1900*, exh. cat. (West Palm Beach, Fla.: Eaton Fine Art, 1996), pp. 12, 15.

70. Stebbins, *The Life and Works of Martin Johnson Heade*, pp. 42-56.

71. Johnson, "Martin Johnson Heade's Salt Marshes and the American Sublime," pp. 34-39.

72. David C. Miller, *Dark Eden: The Swamp in Nineteenth-Century American Culture* (New York: Cambridge University Press, 1989), pp. 1, 17. Miller's important book also introduces us (in its penultimate chapter) to the work of the American poet Frederick Goddard Tuckerman (1821-1873); he persuasively identifies Tuckerman and Heade as "kindred spirits" in their shared love of "desert places," their sensuality, melancholy, and their sense of isolation (pp. 224-240).

73. Sweeney, "A 'very peculiar' Picture: Martin Johnson Heade's *Thunderstorm Over Narragansett Bay*" (as in n. 41), p. 4.

74. See Roger B. Stein, *Seascape and the American Imagination* (New York: Clarkson N. Potter, 1975), where Stein writes that Heade's *Thunder Storm on Narragansett Bay* "can be seen as a secularized version of Cole's *Old Age*" (p. 51).

75. David C. Miller, "The Iconology of Wrecked or Stranded Boats in Mid to Late Nineteenth-Century American Culture," in David C. Miller, ed., *American Iconology: New Approaches to Nineteenth-Century Art and Literature* (New Haven and London: Yale University Press, 1993), pp. 186–208.

76. Miller, "The Iconology of Wrecked or Stranded Boats in Mid to Late Nineteenth-Century American Culture," pp. 205, 208.

77. Sarah Cash, "Singing Beach, Manchester: Four Newly Identified Paintings of the Northern Shore of Massachusetts by Martin Johnson Heade," *American Art Journal* 27, nos. 1–2 (1995–96), pp. 84–98. Cash credits Robert G. Workman for his identification of the site of *Dawn* (cat. 5) as Singing Beach, Manchester, Massachusetts.

78. Sarah Cash, *Ominous Hush: The Thunderstorm Paintings of Martin Johnson Heade*, exh. cat. (Fort Worth, Tex.: Amon Carter Museum, 1994).

79. Ibid., p. 50.

80. See *Catalogue of a Collection of Valuable Oil Paintings: The Property of the Rev. Henry Ward Beecher*, sale cat. (New York: D. V. Ives & Co. at the Derby Gallery, June 3, 1863).

81. Henry Ward Beecher, "The Storm and Its Lessons," in *Sermons by Henry Ward Beecher*, vol. 1 (New York: Harper and Brothers, 1868), p. 228.

82. John Updike, "Heade Storms," *New York Review of Books*, January 12, 1995, p. 8.

THE DEVELOPMENT OF MARTIN JOHNSON HEADE'S PAINTING TECHNIQUE

FEW NINETEENTH-CENTURY ARTISTS had as long or as varied a career as did Martin Johnson Heade. During his teens he began his life as a portrait painter; then, in his late thirties, he started a successful second career as a creator of evocative landscapes. In the same period he quickly developed into one of the best still-life painters of the Victorian era. He continued painting both landscapes and flowers, sometimes synthesizing both in his beautiful studies of hummingbirds, until his death in 1904. Heade adapted his style and technique to each of his subjects while developing a unique and distinctive touch, which unifies his work from beginning to end. Through a study of paintings dated between 1839 and 1872, most from the collection of the Museum of Fine Arts, Boston, I will attempt to describe the evolution of his style, observing changes in his aesthetic approach as well as his methods and materials. My study is based on viewing the paintings in various settings under both normal and ultraviolet light. I also used a binocular microscope to observe the structure and brushwork of the paintings and infrared reflectography (IRR) to discover changes and underdrawing not apparent to the naked eye.[1]

Heade began his painting career in the 1830s as an apprentice to Edward Hicks. By 1839, at the age of twenty, he was painting portraits. His earliest known work is an 1839 portrait of an unidentified woman (see fig. 1). Apart from the basic training he had received from Hicks and possibly some from Edward Hicks's cousin Thomas Hicks (who painted a portrait of the young Heade in the early 1840s (see fig. 35),[2] Heade had no academic training.

Portrait of a Man (fig. 24) is signed in the lower left corner *M. J. Heed 1840*. In this early attempt, Heade struggled to depict the sitter accurately, using a simple, very direct technique. He tried to copy the details and structure of the sitter's face and place it in a fantasized, but conventional, setting. He rendered one element at a time, often losing sight of the whole composition and even of proper proportion. The man's anatomy is distorted and is painted without much confidence. For example, the sitter's hand (or half a hand, to be more literal) and arm are much too large. With the aid of IRR one can see that Heade struggled with the size and shape of the sitter's ear as well as with the eyes. Even with the changes, the sitter's eyes are not in proper relation to one another. One senses the great effort this painting must have been for the young artist.

Local textures in this portrait are not well described. With the exception of an obvious highlight here and there, the artist made no painterly attempt to distinguish the silk of the vest from the man's skin or the walls of the room. The sitter's eyes, although intense, are not moist and the hair seems wooden. However, even in this early work Heade displays a surprising

Fig. 24. *Portrait of a Man*, 1840, oil on canvas. Museum of Fine Arts, Boston, Gift of Lucille Talmud Turecki, 1995.791.

Fig. 25. *Mary Rebecca Clark*, 1857, oil on canvas. Museum of Fine Arts, Boston, Gift of Maxim Karolik for the M. and M. Karolik Collection of American Paintings, 1815–1865, 48.426.

talent for depicting pictorial space, a strength the artist maintained throughout his career. The background recedes convincingly, and there is a credible separation between the sitter and the interior space. Heade achieved this illusion by precisely placing various compositional elements. For example, he slightly adjusted the bases of the columns; carefully juxta-

posed warmer and cooler colors; believably modeled the sitter and columns in three dimensions; introduced a consistent logic in the way light falls within the picture; and, by feathering and softly defining outlines, was moderately successful in capturing an atmospheric quality.

The canvas Heade chose is a medium-weight linen fabric,

which has a commercially applied, cream-colored double ground containing lead white and chalk. No underdrawing is detected. He painted the face first, leaving a reserve for the hair, then filled in the background and the clothing. In this portrait Heade used a cool palette with a few warmer earth tones. The vest is painted using mostly Prussian blue and bone black; the skin is lead white and vermilion; and the background green is a combination of Prussian blue and yellow ocher. Heade's brushwork is labored and heavy with few scumbles and no glazes. Although he has not yet developed a personal style or variety in his brushwork, we do see the beginnings of a formation of his palette, with an inclination toward cooler tones and rudimentary commalike brushstrokes (especially in the hair), which will be developed into a distinctive, calligraphic touch in the later pictures, especially in the orchids and hummingbirds.

During the 1840s and early 1850s Heade may be described as an itinerant portrait painter who occasionally produced genre scenes and landscapes. Over these two decades, he evolved into a confident portraitist. In 1857 Heade painted a portrait of Mary Rebecca Clark (fig. 25), a much more sophisticated and academic painting than the 1840 *Portrait of a Man*. In the seventeen years between these two pictures, Heade had lived in Rome in 1848–49, had seen London and Paris, and had exhibited portraits, genre scenes, and a few landscapes in New York, Brooklyn, St. Louis, Philadelphia, and several other American cities.[3] He had certainly been exposed to great works of art and had met many contemporary painters. With these experiences he had slowly matured as an artist and had attained a distinctive personal style by the late fifties.

The portrait of Mary Rebecca Clark is atmospheric, while her expression has an intensity, especially in the eyes, reminiscent of the 1840 portrait. The background of the portrait is an aura of colors composed mostly of iron oxides. Heade successfully places the believable three-dimensional sitter before this generalized surface. The drawing seems confident and the anatomy is accurate.

The canvas is medium weight. The commercially applied, cream-colored ground does not completely hide the texture of the fabric. Heade began this portrait by sketching the figure in graphite on the ground layer; the drawing is partially visible around the nose and eyes. He seems to have executed the portrait in one sitting, as is suggested by the lack of a reserve for the hair and the paint's having been applied wet into wet. Unlike that of the earlier portrait, the handling of paints is apparent and draws attention to the artist's procedure. The display of the layered structure of the painting and its conspicuous brushwork serve to remind the viewer that, along with its being a portrait of a fourteen-year-old girl, this is a spontaneous creation.

Heade's brushwork in *Mary Rebecca Clark* is varied: there are very tight and blended areas in the skin tones and broad transparent strokes in the sitter's dress. The edge of the collar is painted using a very small, stiff brush, with which he applied a series of little daubs of pastose lead white, creating a light, airy passage of lace with depth and variation. We see here for the first time a technique Heade used in depicting crests of waves during the early 1860s and the frills of orchid petals later in his career. For the sitter's hair Heade employed long strokes of dark brown paint, composed of iron oxide and a bone black, very lightly scumbled over her forehead (a blend of lead white and vermilion), creating the illusion of space around the fine hair. Reflected light from the white collar is seen illuminating the area under her chin. Heade defined variations in dress and

Fig. 26. *Rocks in New England*, 1855, oil on canvas. Museum of
Fine Arts, Boston, Gift of Maxim Karolik for the M. and M. Karolik
Collection of American Paintings, 1815–1865, 47.1171.

Fig. 27. Detail of fig. 26.

hair, not so much with changes of hue, but with variation in the brushwork, allowing the ground color to play an active role. Here, unlike the earlier portrait, transparent reddish brown glazes define the eyelids, brows, and irises of the eyes. Light falls convincingly into the eyes and is reflected off the irises and also the transparent lens.

For Heade the mid-1850s through early 1863 was a time for experimentation and exploration of many different styles and subjects. His interest turned toward landscape. He explored pastures, seashores, wooded scenes, and salt marshes, a subject he would continue to paint for the rest of his life.

In the landscapes of 1855–58 Heade took a step back from the technical mastery he displayed in the portraits of the time. His brushwork in the landscapes is less fluid and has relatively less variety. His uneasiness with the new subject brought to the fore a need for restraint and control.[4]

Rocks in New England (fig. 26), dated 1855, is a medium-sized (17 x 27 in.) horizontal landscape painted on a twill-weave canvas with a commercially applied off-white ground composed mainly of lead white, which hides the canvas texture. The sky occupies the top third of the canvas. The horizon is broken by a single tree, which reaches from the left foreground into the sky. The painting has an aerial perspective as if the artist were painting from one prospect overlooking a road and stone wall to another rocky prospect and beyond across an inland bay. In the foreground and into the middle ground, every rock, leaf, and twig is carefully rendered, as though Heade were following to the letter Asher B. Durand's instruction to a young landscapist made that year in the *Crayon*: "Let him scrupulously accept *whatever* she presents him until he, in a degree, becomes intimate with her infinity . . . , but never let him profane her sacredness by a willful departure from truth."[5]

Durand further advises the artist to *imitate* the details in the foreground while merely *representing* the various flora and fauna in the middle ground and background, allowing the shroud of atmosphere to mute the contrast and color as one's eye moves back in perspective.[6] In the foreground Heade paints each leaf and the yellow flower stalk of the two mulleins (fig. 27) and meticulously renders each stone in the serpentine stone wall. The brushwork follows the contour of each element. The colors in the foreground are relatively bright and pure; the greens are a combination of emerald green, chrome green, and perhaps viridian in combination with yellow earth pigments and some chrome yellow. The ox and the sheep in the middle ground are less detailed with more gentle shadows, and the background is soft with long horizontal brushstrokes of bluish gray.

Contrary to M. E. Chevreul's newly translated color theories,[7] Durand advised in more traditional terms that the landscapist should not adulterate the glories of nature with the addition of randomly selected pure colors to enliven the composition.[8] Heade seems to follow Durand's advice closely in adhering to the natural colors found in the landscape and not venturing to add unobserved color. His palette is generally cool with very few oranges or warm reds. The leaves are depicted in limited shades of pure green with very little addition of other hues for variation. Some yellow is added to the foliage to suggest the light of the sun touching the leaves. The rocks are gray with black shadows, as are the tree trunks.

For visual interest Heade relies solely on the natural variation within the landscape portrayed, with no "tricks of impasto or meaningless glazes," as Durand had suggested.[9] Heade's brushwork, a means to an end in describing the details of nature, is deliberate and methodical. The paint is pastose with

Fig. 28. *The Swing: Children in the Woods*, 1858, oil on canvas. Private Collection, New York.

Fig. 29. Detail of fig. 28.

very few attempts at glazing, the only exception being in the transparent brown shadows used to define the anatomy of the ox and some of the foreground shadows of the bushes and trees.

Heade constructed the painting by first laying in the sky, then the middle ground and foreground, adding details after the composition was set. He left no reserves for the trees or animals, which are placed over the finished landscape. Heade adjusted the size and position of the mullein leaves and of the

legs of the ox, indicating, as in his 1840 portrait, his concern for exact placement and compositional balance.

Unlike the established members of the Hudson River School, including Cole, Durand, Church, Kensett, Gifford, and Bierstadt, who used drawings and oil sketches to plan compositions,[10] Heade's method was to construct the broad landscape setting on the canvas and then to embellish the scene by adding, moving, and/or removing various compositional elements such as animals, staffage, haystacks, flowers, or even hummingbirds.[11] This method allowed Heade to fine-tune the composition as he worked to establish near perfect pictorial harmony. This exactitude coupled with a generally cool palette and limited, often repetitive brushwork give the landscapes and still lifes a surreal, cerebral quality. Heade followed this pattern of construction throughout his career.

In 1858, a year after he painted Mary Rebecca Clark, Heade painted *The Swing: Children in the Woods* (fig. 28), a small woodland scene of two children playing on a swing in a glade. *The Swing* is painted on a medium-weave, 11½-by-15¼-inch canvas with a cream-colored ground. There is no evidence of underdrawing. Here the brushwork and the use of color are radically different from Heade's earlier work and very similar to the working methods of Church, whom he met in late 1858. Unlike the subdued "natural" color scheme of *Rocks in New England*, in *The Swing* the foreground is mostly brown with an occasional touch of bright green to indicate foliage, while the middle ground and trees have been painted with broad, sweeping strokes of color defined with local daubs of bright pure hues, often contrasting. Clusters of bright red, yellow, orange, green, and blue are distributed around the composition to unify it and create points of interest from which one's eye can move to and fro (fig. 29). This method of enlivening the surface with clusters of pure color is exactly the way Church constructed paintings in 1858, such as *Cayambe* (figs. 30, 31). Like many of Church's earlier landscapes, and in keeping with Chevreul's "harmony of contrasts," the sky has a heavy salmon-colored underlayer, which breaks through in many areas, intensifying the blue of the sky.

Another artistic device in this early landscape is thick light-colored impasto glazed with transparent color located on the red highlight on the girl's dress. In this case Heade used one of his favorite transparent pigments, rose madder. This application of paint forms a jewel-like passage by allowing the light to pass through the glassy red tint to reflect off the bright underpaint, charging the color with luminosity. Heade captured light in this way throughout his career to depict the radiance of sunsets with transparent yellows and rose madder, to render the iridescence of hummingbird feathers and butterfly wings with viridian, rose madder, and Prussian blue, and to imitate the translucency of orchid flowers again with rose madder. This method of glazing was uncommon in American paintings at the time and certainly was never a significant part of Church's repertoire. However, it was freely exploited by the Pre-Raphaelites, especially Ford Madox Brown and John Everett Millais.[12] Heade probably saw paintings by Brown and other Pre-Raphaelites at the important *Exhibition of British Art* either in New York in late 1857 or at the Boston Athenaeum in early 1858.[13]

The roots of Heade's mature style can be seen in this painting, which may have been executed shortly after he moved into the Tenth Street Studio Building in New York in November 1858. Even in this small and enclosed composition Heade gives a real sense of pictorial depth. One's eye can move in and around the trees, and the implication of distance beyond the trees is effective. The painter makes fine adjustments in the size and position of the trees and the two figures. Along with the glazed impasto passages, Heade represents branches of trees by linking a series of progressively smaller calligraphic J-shaped strokes, which can be contrasted with Kensett's straight comet-shaped daubs of the time, Gifford's rounder, more globular strokes, or Church's light and infinitely variable touches. As in Heade's later depictions of seaweed on the beach

Fig. 30. Frederic Edwin Church (1826–1900), *Cayambe*, 1858, oil on canvas. Museum of Fine Arts, Boston, Gift of Martha C. Karolik for the M. and M. Karolik Collection of American Paintings, 1815–1865, 47.1237.

Fig. 31. Detail of fig. 30.

in *Shore Scene: Point Judith* (fig. 33) and *Approaching Thunder Storm* (cat. 1), highlights on the log in the foreground are candy striped with swirls of two distinct pigments, a technique that relies on optical mixing in the eye of the viewer for the perceived hue. Heade also used these candy-cane mixes in the hummingbirds of the seventies and in his flower still lifes.

From late 1858 through late 1862, Heade resided first in New York at the Tenth Street Studio Building and later in Boston. He developed an artistic sensibility strongly aligned with the Pre-Raphaelite aesthetic, with bold transparent coloring on a bright ground layer, dramatic lighting, and a zealous description of detail. During these five years Heade's palette evolved from a traditional early-nineteenth-century array based on earth pigments, vermilion, and bone black to a modern, more transparent one using paints many of the Pre-Raphaelites preferred, such as rose madder, cadmium yellow, lemon yellow, verdigris, and emerald green.[14]

In a sketchbook of about 1861–76 now owned by the Museum of Fine Arts, Boston, Heade wrote some rare technical notes,[15] presumably copied from an artists' manual or perhaps from a conversation with another artist: "observations on colors / Verdigris — will bear no amalgamation and is uncertain even as a glazing. Lemon yellow — most beautiful color and stands the / test of heat light and mixture. / Cadmium and em. green turns almost black. / Italian pink — beautiful and permanent as a glaze."[16] Along with this palette shift, Heade seems to have experimented with the ground layers, making them more reflective than the commercially available ones. At times he colored the layer to give an overall tone to the picture. Paintings from this time such as *Dawn* (cat. 5) and *Lake George* (cat. 20) often display craquelure patterns related to slow-drying grounds.

Heade painted *Rhode Island Shore* (see fig. 3) in 1858. As in *Mary Rebecca Clark*, Heade began the composition by drawing a sketch on the prepared canvas. (From this time to the end of his career Heade employed various kinds of underdrawing. He used different media, such as graphite, black ink, brown paint, red ink or red paint, and what appears to be charcoal, at different times and for different subjects.)

Although the general color scheme in the picture is still true to Durand's cool, "truthful" palette, Heade added rose madder glazes in the flowers at the lower left, lemon yellow, Prussian blue, and chrome green in the grass, and emerald green and cadmium in the foliage of the trees. The next year Heade painted *Approaching Thunder Storm* (cat. 1) using essentially the same modern palette. The foreground grasses are carefully portrayed using what appears to be lemon yellow. The brilliant lime green of the midground seems to be a color composed of Prussian blue, cadmium yellow, and lemon yellow found in other paintings of the period.[17]

In 1862 Heade painted *Lake George* (cat. 20) and *Dawn* (cat. 5) and the still life *Roses and Heliotrope in a Vase on a Marble Tabletop* (cat. 26) using the modern palette found in *Rhode Island Shore*. By applying a bright, thick oil ground on top of the commercially prepared canvas in *Dawn* and *Lake George*, Heade increased the reflectance of the ground, thereby illuminating the whole composition.[18] Using a graphite pencil, he drew the horizon, mountains, and the distinguishing features of each landscape. He carefully drew the vase and table lines in *Roses and Heliotrope* using a ruler and some mechanical device such as a compass for the arcs of the vase and a center line to ensure symmetry. In each of these paintings Heade portrays a clear, serene atmosphere with an orderly illumination using a tight range of values with low contrast and muted tones. He models the shapes of the boat in the foreground of *Lake George* and the vase in the still life with the same infinite gradations of light coupled with precise drawing. In the foreground of *Lake George*, he has taken Church's idea of bold clusters of color and softened the effect by creating broader zones of pink, yellow, and blue yet still applying small related touches of more brilliant hues, which are unrelated to the natural colors of the landscape. This can be seen in the reflections on the water of the man and boat in the foreground (fig. 32).

In keeping with Pre-Raphaelite practice, Heade carefully describes each detail in the foreground of *Dawn* and *Lake George*. Each tree, shrub, and mushroom has an individual character. In a seamless gradation to the horizon, Heade represents broader and broader areas. He follows the same practice with the more distinct and brilliant colors in the foreground. In contrast, Church, Kensett, and the other members of the Hudson River School tended to divide their compositions into distinct stages, distinguishing with their brushwork foreground from middle ground, middle ground from background. Heade would adopt this staged method by the late sixties and early seventies, as seen in both his marsh scenes and orchid compositions. Also in contrast to Church, Kensett, and Bierstadt, Heade generally did not use predominantly strong, warm colors such as burnt sienna, yellow ocher, or warm browns in the foreground, opting for the cooler lemon yellow, rose madder, and Prussian blue. This has the effect of distancing the viewer from the scene, creating a less animate, more contemplative ambiance.

In addition, Heade's typical adjustments of compositional elements can be seen in each of these pictures. For example, in *Lake George* a fully painted sailboat just above and to the right of the man in the foreground was eliminated as the work was

Fig. 32. Detail of *Lake George* (cat. 20).

Fig. 33. *Shore Scene: Point Judith*, 1863, oil on canvas. Museum of Fine Arts, Boston, Gift of Mary Harris Clark, 1991.967.

being completed; doubtless Heade decided that open water in that area would serve his purpose better.

In *The Stranded Boat* (cat. 7) Heade moved away from the Pre-Raphaelites by expressing mood and atmosphere. Although Heade painted the shoreline with the formal quiet of *Lake George* and the boat on the beach as a still life with geometric precision and the soft subdued coloring of the vase in *Roses and Heliotrope*, the choice of painting a misty morning with the fog lingering offshore was not conducive to expressing a dramatically lit landscape rich in detail.

For *The Stranded Boat* Heade chose a relatively coarse double-weft fabric and prepared the canvas with a thin ground layer, which allowed the texture of the fabric to remain visible. The picture has an underdrawing, and there are several compositional changes in the paint layers. Although the transition from foreground to middle ground is smooth, there is an abrupt broadening of the brushwork from the trees and rocks

Fig. 34. *Hunters Resting*, 1863, oil on canvas. Museum of Fine Arts, Boston, Gift of Maxim Karolik for the M. and M. Karolik Collection of American Paintings, 1815–1865, 47.1139.

in the middle ground to the veiled trees at the horizon. His palette remained the same as in *Lake George*; lemon yellow, emerald green, Prussian blue, vermilion, zinc white, lead white, and iron-based earth tones have all been identified. This is one of his few paintings without any evidence of rose madder. He painted bits of seaweed on the shore with long strokes of lime green paint composed of Prussian blue and lemon yellow. The branches of the trees are painted with the familiar hooked brushwork.

Later in 1863, in paintings such as *Shore Scene, Point Judith* (fig. 33) and *Hunters Resting* (fig. 34), Heade began to paint with veils of color, leaving broad areas of transparent darks in the shadows and rose madder, Prussian blue, and other transparent glazes over large portions of the skies. He used more oil in his paints, which allowed more subtle mixing of the colors on the canvas and more expressive handling and working wet into wet. He was becoming both more painterly and more proficient.

After traveling to Brazil in 1863, on to England in 1864, and then to Nicaragua in 1866, Heade moved back to the Tenth Street Studio Building in New York. He painted *April Showers* (cat. 21) in the spring of 1868. On the ground layer Heade drew the horizon with what appears to be graphite and painted a dark gray-brown imprimatura over areas that would be darker in the completed painting, such as the right side of the sky and the left foreground. Using the same modern palette he had employed since the late fifties, including lemon yellow, emerald green, cadmium, vermilion, Prussian blue, and rose madder among others, he painted one of his freshest and most original compositions.

Unlike the landscapes of 1862–63, this painting does not make extensive use of glazes. Each hill has a different level of detail, which has the effect of carrying the eye back into space. It is not a continuous perspective as can be seen in *Lake George* or *Shore Scene: Point Judith*. It would seem that varying his brushwork from one area to another became important to Heade at this time.

Using broad, blended strokes of a rather stiff, flat half-inch brush, he painted pink, yellow, blue, and gray areas of the sky. Each color is mixed to give the impression of sunlight passing through low clouds of various densities. As in *The Stranded Boat* Heade was careful to soften the definition of each cloud to create the feeling of a moisture-laden atmosphere. To give the illusion of distance Heade painted the farthest hill light blue-gray with very little color modulation and no impasto. The next line of hills sets the horizon along much of the left side of the composition. Although darker, it has the same light gray underpaint of the more distant hill; however, to indicate the texture of trees in the distance, Heade added some darker green, lighter gray-green, and dark gray in short, choppy quarter-inch strokes. These hills follow the drawn horizon except where they deviate, to exaggerate the silhouette of the hills and lend drama to the whole scene. He also distinguished

fields in this area with long yellow-green brushstrokes that follow the slopes of the hills. To add pictorial depth Heade cast these hills in shadow.

Toward the foreground, the details are more in focus, local color is denoted, hue and contrast are increased. The uncultivated field in the left foreground has a variety of wildflowers, some with bright pink and yellow blooms. He employed brushwork to define textural regions of the composition. Heade used long, smooth strokes in the water and in the more distant, cultivated fields, opposed to short, choppy strokes of thick paint in the trees on the hills and the apple trees. As in the midground fields of *April Showers*, Heade painted the lowlands in many of his marsh scenes from the sixties using long, horizontal brushstrokes of alternating colors. In the middle ground and foreground brushwork follows the contours of details, such as the ox and man tilling the field in the center, the orange haystack, and the trunks of the willows by the stream. To increase the contrast in the foreground, Heade brushed a very wet dark green over the shadows in the trees located just to the left of the willows on the stream bank. This paint reticulated and dried like beads of water on glass. This seems to be an intentional effect because the reticulation would have happened immediately and could have been removed if unwanted; it can be found in many paintings including the orchids and hummingbirds.

In *Cattleya Orchid and Three Brazilian Hummingbirds* (cat. 57), dated 1871, one can see the beaded paint on the right in the middle-ground trees on the horizon line. In this work, which is very loosely painted, Heade rendered the tropical hills schematically with loose, gestured brushstrokes made with a stiff brush loaded with opaque colors. The sky is painted with a broad brush, and the paint is highly blended with very soft transitions from color to color. Heade used transparent glazes only in the orchid flower, the dark brown shadows of the hills behind the hummingbirds, and in the hummingbirds themselves.

Although he lamented the increasing popularity of the French style, from the 1872 until his death in 1904 Heade's basic technique did not change. He generally used underdrawing along the horizon and for some of the major compositional elements. His palette remains the same. However, perhaps in response to impressionism or because he was getting older, his brushwork gradually became more varied, free, and less precise. He also used local glazing less frequently, as he came to rely on a more direct, single application of paint. With the notable exception of the magnolias and the Cherokee roses, Heade painted many of the later paintings more broadly and schematically than the earlier works.

As we see even from this cursory examination, Heade in his early years, up to the mid-1860s, was constantly searching for a technique that would allow him to express his own vision. Just as he continually tried out different subjects, so he experimented in a unique way with a wide variety of methods and materials.

JIM WRIGHT

NOTES

I am very grateful for the collaboration and keen insight of Theodore E. Stebbins, Jr., John Moors Cabot Curator of American Paintings; Janet L. Comey, Curatorial Assistant; Karen E. Quinn, Research Fellow, all in the Paintings Department of the Museum of Fine Arts, Boston; Jean Woodward, Associate Conservator of Paintings at the MFA; and Elizabeth Leto Fulton, a conservator in private practice in the Boston area, who has been studying the MFA's collection of Heades for the last two years with the support of the Samuel H. Kress Foundation. In December 1993 Kate Duffy, Advanced Level Intern in the Scientific Research Department at the Museum of Fine Arts, Boston, under the supervision of Richard Newman, Research Scientist, completed an unpublished report of the technical analysis of twenty Heade paintings. Several areas on each painting were quantitatively analyzed using nondestructive X-ray fluorescence, yielding elemental data on each. From this data tentative pigment identification is possible. In February 1998 Leto Fulton started a Kress–Foundation funded study of cross sections from Heade paintings in the MFA collection under the joint supervision of Richard Newman and me. This study, which included microscopic examination of the samples and microprobe analysis of the pigments, yielded more information confirming the identification of certain pigments and giving insight into the layered structure of the paint and ground layers.

1. Infrared reflectography uses a video camera sensitive to infrared radiation to see preliminary drawing and underlayers of paint.
2. Theodore E. Stebbins, Jr., *The Life and Works of Martin Johnson Heade* (New Haven, Conn.: Yale University Press, 1975), pp. 3–6.
3. Ibid., p. 13.
4. For some reason he did not experience the same uneasiness with his first still lifes in the early 1860s as he did with landscapes. Perhaps it was because the subject was less fleeting, more like portraiture. The genre was less well established and the competition perhaps less intense.
5. Asher B. Durand, "Letters on Landscape Painting: Letter 1," *Crayon* 1 (January 3, 1855), p. 2. There are many links to Heade in the *Crayon*; see Stebbins, *Martin Johnson Heade*, p. 29.

6. Durand, "Letter 5" (March 7, 1855), pp. 145-146.

7. M. E. Chevreul, *La Loi du Contraste simultané des couleurs* (Paris: Pitois-Levrault, 1839). Translated to English in 1854 by Charles Martel. John Wiley of New York advertised an English translation in *Crayon* 1 (January 3, 1855), p. 48.

8. Durand, "Letter 1," p. 2.

9. Ibid.

10. See Eleanor Jones Harvey, *The Painted Sketch: American Impressions from Nature, 1830–1880*, exh. cat. (New York: Harry N. Abrams, in association with the Dallas Museum of Art, 1998), pp. 25-61, for an excellent description of the use of the sketch by artists in the Hudson River School.

11. Winslow Homer also used this method of composition in many of his oil paintings and watercolors.

12. Libby Shelden, "Methods and Materials of the Pre-Raphaelite Circle in the 1850s," in Ashok Roy and Perry Smith, eds., *Painting Techniques: History, Materials, and Studio Practice* (London: International Institute of Conservation, 1998), pp. 229-234; and Stephen Hackney, "John Everett Millais, *Ophelia, 1851–52*," pp. 74-79, and "William Holman Hunt, *The Awakening Conscience*," pp. 80-85, in "Stephen Hackney, Rica James, and Joyce Townsend, eds., *Paint and Purpose: A Study of Technique in British Art* (London: Tate Gallery Publishing, 1999).

13. Stebbins, *Martin Johnson Heade*, p. 39.

14. See Shelden.

15. Stebbins, *Martin Johnson Heade*, p. 288, and Sarah Cash, *Ominous Hush: The Thunderstorm Paintings of Martin Johnson Heade*, exh. cat. (Fort Worth, Tex.: Amon Carter Museum, 1994).

16. See R. D. Harley, *Artists' Pigments, c. 1600–1835: A Study in English Documentary Sources*, 2d ed. (London: Butterworth Scientific, 1982), for a full characterization and history of each of the pigments.

Verdigris: bluish transparent, basic copper acetate (p. 80)
Emerald green or *Scheinfurt green:* bright green copper aceto-arsenite (p. 84)
Lemon yellow: greenish in color either barium chromate or strontium chromate (p. 103)
Cadmium yellow: cadmium sulfide (p. 103)
Italian pink: organic yellow, dull yellow or yellow-brown from yellow berries or weld or later quercitron bark (black or yellow oak) dye cast onto a substrate such as aluminum silicate (p. 115)

17. For a technical description of the painting, see Cash, *Ominous Hush*, pp. 73-74.

18. Most of the paintings from this period have extensive drying cracks in some areas, which were probably caused by the slow drying of the thick upper ground layer.

1819 Martin Johnson Heed was born on August 11, in Lumberville, Bucks County, Pa., the eldest child of Joseph Cowell Heed and Sarah Johnson Heed. He lived in Bucks County until about 1842.

c. 1837–39 He studied in Newtown, Bucks County, Pa., with Edward Hicks and possibly also the young Thomas Hicks, who painted Heade's portrait around this time (fig. 35).

1839 Heade painted his earliest extant work, *Portrait of a Young Lady* (see fig. 1).

1841 His first exhibited work, *Portrait of a Little Girl* (unlocated), was shown at the Pennsylvania Academy of the Fine Arts in Philadelphia. Heade continued to exhibit occasionally at the Academy until 1868.

1843 Heade moved to New York, where he exhibited at the National Academy of Design for the first time. He exhibited there again in 1852, then regularly between 1859 and 1890.

1844 He moved to Trenton, N.J.

Fig. 35. Thomas Hicks (1823–1890), *Martin Johnson Heade*, about 1840–42, oil on canvas. Bucks County Historical Society.

1845 Heade moved to Brooklyn, N.Y., then Richmond, Va., where he painted portraits.

1846 Heade lived in Richmond, Va., at least through February. He was also probably in Washington, D.C. At about this time he changed the spelling of his name to "Heade."

He painted General Samuel Houston (see fig. 2).

Fig. 36. *Portrait of the Artist's Sister*, about 1848–52, oil on canvas. Private Collection.

1847 Heade returned to Trenton; he then moved to Philadelphia (the *Philadelphia Directory* listed him as "M. J. Heade, portrait painter, S. W. 8th and Mulberry").

He exhibited for the only time at the American Art-Union in New York this year; his entry was a genre picture, *Sleepy Fisherman* (unlocated).

Fig. 37. *The Roman Newsboys*, 1848, oil on canvas. The Toledo Museum of Art, Toledo, Ohio, Gift of Florence Scott Libbey, 53.68.

Fig. 38. *Commodore Oliver Hazard Perry — Copy from Jarvis*, 1855, oil on canvas. James DeWolf Perry, Stockbridge, Mass. (on loan to the National Portrait Gallery, Washington, D.C.).

Fig. 39. *Bishop Thomas March Clark*, about 1856, oil on canvas. The Rhode Island Historical Society, Providence, R.I., Gift of Bishop Thomas March Clark, 1890, 1890.3.1.

1848–50 By January 1848 Heade had left for Rome; he also visited England and France.

In 1849 and 1850 he exhibited a number of paintings at the Western Art Union, Cincinnati, including *The Roman Newsboys* (fig. 37) both years.

1851–53 Heade was living in St. Louis.

1853–54 Heade moved to Chicago. Late in 1853 he visited Madison, Wisc.

1854–56 Heade moved back to Trenton.

1855 He visited Bristol, R.I.; he painted *Rocks in New England*, his earliest dated landscape (see fig. 26).

1856 Heade moved to Providence, R.I. *Scene on Narragansett Bay*, his first exhibited landscape, was shown at the Pennsylvania Academy.

1857 By late June, Heade was in New York. He visited North Conway, N.H., in July and

August. In September, he worked at his father's in Lumberville, Pa., and visited Trenton. In December, he was in Montgomery, Ala.

He exhibited at the Boston Athenaeum for the first time, showing *Commodore Perry — Copy from Jarvis* (fig. 38), *Portrait* [Bishop Clark] (fig. 39), and *View on the Narragansett Bay*. He would regularly show there through the end of the decade, then sporadically in the 1860s, and for the last time in 1873.

1858 Between January and April, Heade traveled to Demopolis, Ala., Mobile, Ala. and New Orleans. In May he was in Chicago and by about June in Providence, at 34 North Main. He spent September in Bristol, R.I., and in November he moved to New York, to 15 10th Street (Tenth Street Studio Building).

1859 Heade lived in New York and in early May visited New Haven, Conn.

He painted his earliest dated marsh scene (fig. 40), as well as *Approaching Thunder Storm* (cat. 1).

He also exhibited at Williams and Everett, Boston art dealers, for the first time; he would continue to exhibit there frequently until 1863, and occasionally thereafter.

1860 Heade moved to Providence. His Providence dealer, through 1865, was Seth M. Vose. In early June he was in Boston. In July he traveled to the Thousand Islands in the St. Lawrence River and to Burlington, Vt., on Lake Champlain, and to the White Mountains in New Hampshire; in August he was probably in Newport.

1861 By the fall Heade had moved to Boston, where he remained until 1863. In the summer he probably visited Newport and Manchester, Mass.

Fig. 40. *Marsh at Dawn*, 1859, oil on canvas. Collection of Jerald Dillon Fessenden.

1862 Heade was listed in the *Boston Directory* at 27 Studio Building (at the corner of Tremont and Bromfield Streets); boarding at the Parker House. In July he visited Campobello Island and St. George in Passamaquoddy Bay, New Brunswick, Canada; also nearby Eastport, Me.

1863 Heade painted at Lynn and Newburyport, Mass., and in August at Rye Beach, N.H. He sailed from New York on the *Golden City* on September 2, 1863, arriving in Rio de Janeiro, Brazil, on September 20.

1864 Heade worked in Rio de Janeiro. On March 30 he was awarded the Order of the Rose by Dom Pedro II, emperor of Brazil. On April 8 he sailed for England, arriving there May 5. He stayed at No. 6 Russell Place, Fitzroy Square, London; about October 1, he moved to a studio at 16 Douro Place, Victoria Road, Kensington.

1865 Heade returned to the United States late in the year, going to Providence.

1866 Between June and August he made a brief trip to Nicaragua. By August 10 he was staying in Trenton, with W. R. Clapp. In the early fall he returned to New York, to 15 10th Street (the Studio Building, whose address was changed during the year to 51 West 10th St.), where he occupied Frederic E. Church's studio (no. 7). He began a correspondence with Church that lasted until 1900.

1867–81 Heade worked in New York, subletting Church's studio at 51 West 10th Street; he also had a "very nice sleeping room on 6th Avenue." He usually traveled in the summer months.

1867 He spent the late summer at Point Judith, R.I., and visited Church at Hudson, N.Y., in September.

1868 Heade was elected to the Union League Club, New York.

1869 In early August he visited Cambridge, Mass.; he also traveled to Narragansett Pier and Newport, R.I.

1870 About January 1 Heade sailed for Central America, his third trip to the tropics. From Barranquilla, Colombia, he traveled to Cienega and Santa Marta, then to Colon, Panama; he next sailed to Jamaica, arriving in Kingston on February 24. By mid-May he was back in New York, working on a large painting of Jamaica

(unlocated). He also executed his earliest dated hummingbird and tropical flower painting, *Tropical Landscape with Ten Hummingbirds* (cat. 54).

1871 In July he visited Lake Mohonk in the Shawangunk Mountains, N.Y.

1872 Heade spent the summer in upstate New York: by mid-July he was at Lake George; in August, at Fort Ticonderoga on Lake Champlain; and then in late August, at Lebanon Springs, N.Y.

1873 By mid-July Heade was in Newport; in October he traveled to the Connecticut shore.

1875 March through June Heade traveled overland to San Francisco; by the late summer he was back at the Connecticut shore.

At about this time, he executed *The Prairies* and *Prairie Sunset* (both unlocated).

1876 In early summer he traveled to Manchester, Vt.; in August and September he was in Connecticut.

He exhibited two paintings, *Off the California Coast* and *Flowers* at the Centennial Exposition in Philadelphia (both unlocated).

1877 He spent July in Lebanon Springs, N.Y.

1880 In March Heade's first article for *Forest and Stream* was published; he wrote regularly until August 1883, then began again in 1891, continuing to contribute until a few weeks before his death in September 1904. In the summer he traveled to the Maryland shore.

1881 In early June Heade was in Philadelphia; he spent the summer in Bridgeport, Conn. By November he had moved to Washington, D.C., to a studio in the Corcoran Building; he remained in Washington through the beginning of the next year.

1882 By June Heade was staying at the St. Denis Hotel, at Broadway and 11th Street in New York. In July he traveled to Northampton, Mass.; he also visited Greenfield and Ashland. In August he returned to the St. Denis Hotel. In September he spent a week at Saratoga, N.Y., and then again returned to New York City in September and October. In early November he went quail shooting at the eastern end of Long Island. Later in November he was in Boston, at Young's Hotel; in December he moved to the Maverick House in East Boston.

1883 By March Heade settled in St. Augustine, Fla., after a trip around the state which included stops at Jacksonville, Palatka, Enterprise, Ocala, and Waldo. He remained in St. Augustine for the rest of his life. He purchased a house at 105 San Marco Avenue and was renovating it by mid-April. He spent the fall in New York City, where he and Miss Elizabeth Smith were married on October 9 at the home of William Fitch (547 Madison Avenue; see fig. 41); the ceremony was performed by Bishop Thomas March Clark, whom Heade had known since about 1856 when he painted his portrait in Providence.

He painted his earliest Florida landscape (fig. 42).

1884–1904 Doll and Richards was his Boston dealer. Heade exhibited regularly with Gill's Gallery in Springfield, Mass., and often used James S. Earle & Sons, Philadelphia, as his frame maker.

1885 In June he was planning a trip north by steamer from Charleston, S.C. In September he stayed at 23 East 46th Street, New York.

1886 He painted *The Great Florida Marsh* (fig. 43).

Fig. 41. Mr. and Mrs. Heade in St. Augustine, about late 1880s, photograph. Private Collection.

Fig. 42. *Evening, Lake Alto, Florida*, 1883, oil on canvas. Sam and Robbie Vickers, The Florida Collection.

1887 About June Heade moved into the small studio building that Henry Morrison Flagler had erected behind the Ponce de Leon Hotel. Heade occupied studio number 7 until his death. Heade wrote that he was working on commissions for two large paintings at $2,000 each for Flagler, describing them as "a Jamaica picture, with tree ferns and things" (cat. 24) and "a Florida scene, a sun-set" (fig. 44). He traveled north in the fall.

1904 He executed his last dated paintings. Heade died on September 4 in St. Augustine, leaving all his property to his wife, Elizabeth Smith Heade. He was buried at Evergreen Cemetery in Brooklyn, N.Y.

Fig. 43 (top). *The Great Florida Marsh*, 1886, oil on canvas. Kenan Family.

Fig. 44 (bottom). *The Great Florida Sunset*, 1887, oil on canvas. Private Collection.

CHECKLIST OF THE EXHIBITION

1. *Approaching Thunder Storm*, 1859
Oil on canvas, 28 x 44 in.
The Metropolitan Museum of Art, Gift
of Erving Wolfe Foundation and Mr.
and Mrs. Erving Wolfe, 1975.
(1975.160)

2. *Seascape: Sunrise*, 1860
Oil on canvas, 28 x 50 in.
Private Collection

3. *Seascape: Sunset*, 1861
Oil on canvas, 26 x 44 in.
The Detroit Institute of Arts,
Founders Society Purchase, Robert H.
Tannahill Foundation Fund, 1995.26

4. *Approaching Storm: Beach near
Newport*, about 1861-63
Oil on canvas, 28 x 54 1/4 in.
Museum of Fine Arts, Boston, Gift of
Maxim Karolik for the M. and M.
Karolik Collection of American
Paintings, 1815-1865, 45.889

5. *Dawn*, 1862
Oil on canvas, 12 1/4 x 24 1/4 in.
Museum of Fine Arts, Boston, Gift of
Maxim Karolik for the M. and M.
Karolik Collection of American
Paintings, 1815-1865, 47.1143

6. *Twilight, Singing Beach*, 1863
Oil on canvas, 20 x 36 in.
Fine Arts Museums of San Francisco,
Gift of Mr. and Mrs. John D.
Rockefeller 3rd, 1993.35.12

7. *The Stranded Boat*, 1863
Oil on canvas, 22 7/8 x 36 7/8 in.
Museum of Fine Arts, Boston,
Gift of Maxim Karolik for the M. and
M. Karolik Collection of American
Paintings, 1815-1865, 48.1026

8. *Thunder Storm on Narragansett Bay*,
1868
Oil on canvas, 32 1/8 x 54 3/4 in.
Amon Carter Museum, Fort Worth,
Texas, 1977.17

9. *Becalmed, Long Island Sound*, 1876
Oil on canvas, 15 x 30 in.
Theodore G. and Eleanor S. Congdon

10. *Summer Showers*, about 1866-76
Oil on canvas, 13 1/16 x 25 15/16 in.
Brooklyn Museum of Art, Brooklyn,
New York, Dick S. Ramsay Fund, 47.8

11. *Newburyport Meadows*, about 1871-75
Oil on canvas, 10 1/2 x 22 in.
The Metropolitan Museum of Art,
Purchase, The Charles Engelhard
Foundation Gift, in memory of
Charles Engelhard; Morris K. Jesup,
Maria DeWitt Jesup, and Pfeiffer
Funds; John Osgood and Elizabeth
Amis Cameron Blanchard Memorial
Fund; Thomas J. Watson Gift, by
exchange; and Gifts of Robert E. Tod
and William Gedney Bunce, by
exchange, 1985. (1985.117)

12. *Sunrise on the Marshes*, 1863
Oil on canvas, 26 3/4 x 50 1/4 in.
Collection of the Flint Institute of
Arts, Gift of Mr. and Mrs. William L.
Richards through the Viola E. Bray
Charitable Trust Fund

13. *Sudden Shower, Newbury Marshes*,
about 1866-76
Oil on canvas, 13 1/4 x 26 5/16 in.
Yale University Art Gallery,
Gift of Theodore E. Stebbins, Jr., B.A.
1960, in memory of H. John Heinz, III,
B.A. 1960, and Collection of Mary C.
and James W. Fosburgh, B.A. 1933,
M.A. 1935, by exchange

14. *Salt Marsh Hay*, about 1866–76
Oil on canvas, 13 x 26 in.
The Butler Institute of American Art,
Youngstown, Ohio

15. *The Great Swamp*, 1868
Oil on canvas, $14^{7}/_{8}$ x $30^{1}/_{8}$ in.
Fine Arts Museums of San Francisco,
Gift of Mr. and Mrs. John D.
Rockefeller 3rd, 1993.35.11

16. *Sunset Marsh (Sinking Sun)*, 1868
Oil on canvas, $8^{1}/_{16}$ x $16^{1}/_{16}$ in.
Collection of David L. Long and
Elizabeth Valk Long, New York

17. *Two Fishermen in the Marsh, at
Sunset*, about 1876–82
Oil on canvas, $15^{1}/_{4}$ x $30^{1}/_{4}$ in.
Private Collection

18. *Marshfield Meadows*, about 1877–78
Oil on canvas, $17^{3}/_{4}$ x 44 in.
The Currier Gallery of Art,
Manchester, New Hampshire,
Currier Funds, 1962.13

19. *Hayfields: A Clear Day*, about 1871–80
Oil on canvas, $17^{1}/_{4}$ x 36 in.
Collection of Jo Ann and Julian
Ganz, Jr.

20. *Lake George*, 1862
Oil on canvas, 26 x $49^{3}/_{8}$ in.
Museum of Fine Arts, Boston,
Bequest of Maxim Karolik, 64.430

21. *April Showers*, 1868
Oil on canvas, $19^{7}/_{8}$ x $40^{1}/_{4}$ in.
Museum of Fine Arts, Boston,
Gift of Maxim Karolik for the M. and
M. Karolik Collection of American
Paintings, 1815–1865, 47.1173

22. *Brazilian Forest*, 1864
Oil on canvas, $20^{1}/_{16}$ x 16 in.
Museum of Art, Rhode Island School
of Design, Providence, R.I.,
Gift of Mr. and Mrs. C. Richard
Steedman, 68.052

23. *Sunset: Harbor at Rio*, 1864
Oil on canvas, $20^{1}/_{8}$ x 35 in.
Courtesy of the Museum of American
Art of the Pennsylvania Academy of
the Fine Arts, Philadelphia,
Henry C. Gibson Fund, 1985.10

24. *View from Fern-Tree Walk, Jamaica*,
1887
Oil on canvas, 53 x 90 in.
Manoogian Collection

25. *Trailing Arbutus*, 1860
Oil on canvas, 10 x 20 in.
Lent by Mr. and Mrs. Stuart P. Feld

26. *Roses and Heliotrope in a Vase on a
Marble Tabletop*, 1862
Oil on board, $13^{7}/_{8}$ x $10^{5}/_{8}$ in.
Private Collection

27. *A Vase of Corn Lilies and Heliotrope*,
1863
Oil on canvas, $16^{3}/_{8}$ x $12^{3}/_{8}$ in.
The Saint Louis Art Museum,
Purchase, Eliza McMillan Fund,
68.1965

28. *Wildflowers in a Brown Vase*, about
1860–65
Oil on canvas, $17^{1}/_{2}$ x $13^{1}/_{2}$ in.
Philadelphia Museum of Art, Bequest
of Lisa Norris Elkins, 1950-092-005

29. *Vase of Mixed Flowers*, about 1872
Oil on canvas, $17^{1}/_{4}$ x $13^{1}/_{2}$ in.
Museum of Fine Arts, Boston, Bequest
of Martha C. Karolik for the M. and M.
Karolik Collection of American
Paintings, 1815–1865, 48.427

30. *Red Flower in a Vase*, about 1871–80
Oil on canvas, $15^{1}/_{2}$ x 12 in.
Manoogian Collection

31. *Branch of Apple Blossoms against a
Cloudy Sky*, 1867
Oil on board, 14 x 12 in.
Private Collection

32. *A Spray of Apple Blossoms*, 1870
Oil on canvas, $14^{1}/_{2}$ x $12^{1}/_{4}$ in.
Collection of Mr. and Mrs. Henry
Luce III

33. *Apple Blossoms and Hummingbird*,
1871
Oil on canvas, 14 x 18 in.
Addison Gallery of American Art,
Phillips Academy, Andover,
Massachusetts, Museum purchase,
1945.4

34. *The White Rose*, about 1874–80
Oil on Winsor and Newton artist's
board, 12 x 10 in.
Collection of James and Barbara
Palmer

35. *Ruby-Topaz*, about 1864–65
Oil on canvas, 12 1/4 x 10 in.
Manoogian Collection

36. *Brazilian Ruby*, about 1864–65
Oil on canvas, 12 1/4 x 10 in.
Manoogian Collection

37. *Black-throated Mango*, about 1864–65
Oil on canvas, 12 1/4 x 10 in.
Manoogian Collection

38. *Amethyst Woodstar*, about 1864–65
Oil on canvas, 12 1/4 x 10 in.
Manoogian Collection

39. *Frilled Coquette*, about 1864–65
Oil on canvas, 12 1/4 x 10 in.
Manoogian Collection

40. *Tufted Coquette*, about 1864–65
Oil on canvas, 12 1/4 x 10 in.
Manoogian Collection

41. *Black-breasted Plovercrest*, about
1864–65
Oil on canvas, 12 1/4 x 10 in.
Manoogian Collection

42. *Fork-tailed Woodnymph*, about
1864–65
Oil on canvas, 12 1/4 x 10 in.
Manoogian Collection

43. *Hooded Visorbearer*, about 1864–65
Oil on canvas, 12 1/4 x 10 in.
Manoogian Collection

44. *Crimson Topaz*, about 1864–65
Oil on canvas, 12 1/4 x 10 in.
Manoogian Collection

45. *Stripe-breasted Starthroat*, about
1864–65
Oil on canvas, 12 1/4 x 10 in.
Manoogian Collection

46. *Snowcap*, about 1864–65
Oil on canvas, 12 1/4 x 10 in.
Manoogian Collection

47. *Black-eared Fairy*, about 1864–65
Oil on canvas, 12 1/4 x 10 in.
Manoogian Collection

48. *White-vented Violet-ear*, about
1864–65
Oil on canvas, 12 1/4 x 10 in.
Manoogian Collection

49. *Ruby-throated Hummingbird*, about
1864–65
Oil on canvas, 12 1/4 x 10 in.
Manoogian Collection

50. *Blue Morpho Butterfly*, about 1864–65
Oil on canvas, 12 1/4 x 10 in.
Manoogian Collection

51. *Two Hummingbirds with Their Young*,
about 1864–65
Oil on canvas, 13 x 11 in.
Collection of Jerald Dillon Fessenden

52. *Two Sun Gems on a Branch*, about
1864–65
Oil on canvas, 10 7/8 x 9 in.
Manoogian Collection

53. *Ruby Throat of North America*, 1865
Oil on canvas, 11 3/4 x 9 in.
Private Collection

54. *Tropical Landscape with Ten
Hummingbirds*, 1870
Oil on canvas, 18 x 30 in.
Roy Nutt Family Trust

55. *Two Hummingbirds Perched on
Passion Flower Vines*, about 1870–83
Oil on canvas, 20 x 12 1/4 in.
Private Collection

56. *Passion Flowers and Hummingbirds*, about 1870–83
Oil on canvas, 15½ x 21⅝ in.
Museum of Fine Arts, Boston,
Gift of Maxim Karolik for the M. and
M. Karolik Collection of American
Paintings, 1815–1865, 47.1138

57. *Cattleya Orchid and Three Brazilian Hummingbirds*, 1871
Oil on panel, 13¾ x 18 in.
National Gallery of Art, Washington,
Gift of The Morris and Gwendolyn
Cafritz Foundation, 1982.73.1

58. *Orchid with Two Hummingbirds*, 1871
Oil on panel, 13¾ x 18 in.
Reynolda House, Museum of
American Art, Winston-Salem, North
Carolina

59. *Fighting Hummingbirds with Pink Orchid*, about 1875–90
Oil on canvas, 16¼ x 14⅛ in.
Private Collection, Kingston,
Massachusetts

60. *Two Fighting Hummingbirds with Two Orchids*, 1875
Oil on canvas, 17½ x 27¾ in.
Private Collection

61. *Orchid and Hummingbirds near a Mountain Lake*, about 1875–90
Oil on canvas, 15 3/16 x 20½ in.
Private Collection

62. *Orchids and Hummingbird*, about 1875–83
Oil on canvas, 14⅛ x 22⅛ in.
Museum of Fine Arts, Boston,
Gift of Maxim Karolik for the M. and
M. Karolik Collection of American
Paintings, 1815–1865, 47.1164

63. *An Amethyst Hummingbird with a White Orchid*, about 1875–90
Oil on canvas, 20 x 12⅛ in.
Collection of Jo Ann and Julian
Ganz, Jr.

64. *Study of Lealia Purpurata and Another Orchid*, about 1870
Oil on canvas, 8½ x 13 in.
From the Collection of the
St. Augustine Historical Society

65. *Branches of Cherokee Roses*, about 1883–88
Oil on canvas, 10 x 17 in.
From the Collection of the St.
Augustine Historical Society

66. *Study of Three Blossoms of Magnolia*, about 1883–88
Oil on canvas, 10¼ x 14½ in.
From the Collection of the St.
Augustine Historical Society

67. *White Cherokee Roses in a Salamander Vase*, about 1883–95
Oil on canvas, 26 x 13 in.
Lent by James W. and Frances G.
McGlothlin

68. *A Magnolia on Red Velvet*, about 1885–95
Oil on canvas, 15 x 24 in.
Teresa Heinz and the Late Senator
John Heinz

69. *Two Magnolias and a Bud on Teal Velvet*, about 1885–95
Oil on canvas, 15¼ x 24¼ in.
Lent by James W. and Frances G.
McGlothlin

70. *Giant Magnolias*, about 1885–95
Oil on canvas, 15¼ x 24 in.
The R. W. Norton Art Gallery,
Shreveport, Louisiana

71. *Giant Magnolias on a Blue Velvet Cloth*, about 1885–95
Oil on canvas, 15⅛ x 24 3/16 in.
National Gallery of Art, Washington,
Gift of The Circle of the National
Gallery of Art in Commemoration of
its 10th Anniversary, 1996.14.1

72. *Magnoliae Grandiflorae*, 1888
Oil on canvas, 15 x 24 in.
Collection of Jo Ann and Julian
Ganz, Jr.

73. *Florida River Scene*, about 1887–1900
Oil on canvas, 17 x 35½ in.
Private Collection
[Boston and Washington only]

INDEX

All works of art are by Martin Johnson Heade, unless otherwise noted.

Page numbers in *italics* denote illustrations.

DESIGNED BY SUSAN MARSH

EDITED BY FRONIA W. SIMPSON

COMPOSED IN ITC BODONI BY MATT MAYERCHAK

PRINTED AND BOUND AT CS GRAPHICS PTE LTD, SINGAPORE